Parental Rights:
The Contemporary Assault
on Traditional Liberties

Edited by:
Stephen M. Krason and
Robert J. D'Agostino

Contents

Preface   7
   Stephen M. Krason

The Basis for the Traditional   13
   Rights and Responsibilities of Parents
   Raphael T. Waters

Rights, Real and Ersatz   39
   Kenneth D. Whitehead

School Desegregation Policy: State Disregard   45
   of the Rights of Black and White Parents
   Raymond D. Wolters

Parental Rights and the Life Issues   49
   Thomas J. Marzen

Parental Rights and Education   77
   Charles E. Rice

Classroom Sex Education: 93
   Undermining Parental Rights
   James Likoudis

State Intervention in the Family   115
   and Parental Rights: A Psychological Assessment
   Roger Rinn

State Intervention in the Family   135
   and Parental Rights: A Legal Assessment
   Robert J. D'Agostino

Child Abuse: Pseudo-Crisis,   153
   Dangerous Bureaucrats, Destroyed Families
   Stephen M. Krason

Index   197

Contributors

Raphael T. Waters, D.Ph., is Associate Professor of Philosophy at Niagara University and has contributed articles to *Social Justice Review*, *Linacre Quarterly* and other journals.

Kenneth D. Whitehead is Deputy Assistant Secretary for Higher Education Programs in the U.S. Department of Education and author of *Respectable Killing: The New Abortion Imperative* and other books and articles.

Raymond R. Wolters, Ph.D., is Professor of History at the University of Delaware and author of *The Burden of Brown: Thirty Years of School Desegregation*.

Thomas J. Marzen, Esq., is General Counsel of the National Legal Center for the Medically Dependent and Disabled and Associate Editor of *Issues in Law and Medicine*.

Charles E. Rice, Esq., J.S.D., is Professor of Law at the University of Notre Dame and the author of *The Supreme Court and Public Prayer*, *Beyond Abortion* and other books and articles.

James Likoudis is President of Catholics United for the Faith and the author of many books and articles on religious and educational topics. He has lectured widely on parental rights in education, sex education, religious education, and related topics.

Roger Rinn, Ph.D., is a practicing psychologist in Huntsville, Alabama and former Director of the Huntsville Mental Health Clinic (Children's Division).

Robert J. D'Agostino, Esq., is Legal Advisor to the National Legal Center for the Public Interest, Visiting Scholar at the Center for Judicial Studies and a former law professor.

Stephen M. Krason, Esq., Ph.D., is Assistant Professor of Political Science at the Franciscan University of Steubenville and Adjunct Research Associate of the Intercollegiate Studies Institute. He is the author of *Abortion: Politics, Morality, and the Constitution.*

Acknowledgements

Special thanks are due to the Intercollegiate Studies Institute (ISI), and especially Messrs. E. Victor Milione and John F. Lulves, Jr., for its support of the symposium which generated most of the chapters of this book and of this book project, Mrs. Pat Mangano and the rest of the support staff at ISI for their assistance in typing portions of an earlier draft of the manuscript, Mrs. B.J. Brehm and her staff at the Franciscan University of Steubenville for typing parts of the immediate pre-publication draft of the manuscript, and to Professor Gregory J. Wolfe and his staff at Christendom College Press for their editorial and other work and their kind cooperation which made the final production of this book remarkably rapid and smooth.

Preface

In recent years, numerous public issues have included, directly or indirectly, questions of parental rights. These issues have involved school desegregation, busing, abortion, child abuse legislation and regulations, the provision of contraceptives by governmental and private agencies to minors without parental consent, as well as a myriad of educational policy matters from textbook selection, sex education programs, and values clarification courses to publicly-provided transportation for non-public school students. Legal cases stretch from infanticide of handicapped newborns and the federal government's attempt to stop it to the Equal Rights Amendment, and the list could go on. When one talks about parental rights, one is, of course, really speaking about issues involving the family. This decade's attention to family issues seems to confirm the prediction made some years ago by one prominent participant in family policy controversies that the issue of the Eighties would be the family. The prominence of issues like those above, plus the mounting evidence that the American family is in a troubled state (e.g., the high divorce rate, the large number of single-parent families, the continued serious problem of juvenile delinquency, the growing number of child suicides), make this book on parental rights and its genesis, the April 1984 symposium at The Delaware Law School of Widener University, most timely.

The fact that so many issues involving parental rights and the family have exploded upon the American scene and have generated such a fever-pitch of emotion signals the profound struggle taking place between two competing views of the family. This struggle involves a fundamental disagreement about the proper role and structure of the family, about the proper relationship between spouses and between parents and children, and about whether the family is natural, as men have historically thought, or merely a conventional institution. There is even dispute about what a "family" is. Disagreements over such basics make clear why there has been so little room for compromise on family issues in the political arena. They also demonstrate that the controversy over the family is much more than a political or sociological dispute; it is, at its heart, a metaphysical conflict.

Thus, in reality, this disagreement about the family reflects a disagreement about the nature, source, and destiny of human existence, the existence of a moral order beyond man, and the relationship of man to that order, to God, and to civil society. The reasons for these differing perspectives, and how and why they affect issues of parental rights, are discussed in this book.

The basic questions which stand immediately behind most judicial and public policy controversies on parental rights are also addressed by the papers. Such questions as: What should the role of the state be with regard to the family? What kinds of treatment and behavior should the state reasonably be permitted to require parents to give to or manifest toward their children? When can the state's authority validly supplant parental authority over children? What should be the criteria to determine when the state can intervene in the family? What is the extent of the natural rights of parents that the state must respect and even actively safeguard? What rights do parents have to control their children's education and how are these being infringed upon? How these questions will be answered by our political society will have profound implications for family life in America, as well as for the future nature of our democracy and constitutional liberties.

The Intercollegiate Studies Institute (ISI) has sponsored both this book and the symposium. It is a fitting subject for ISI because it involves the role of the family and its relationship to the state, for the Institute's purpose is to defend and promote the truths of the Western and American tradition on the university campus. This tradition has various components: philosophy, as embodied in the thinking of the classics and those modern thinkers who believe in objective truth and the natural law-natural rights synthesis; theology, as expressed in our Judeo-Christian heritage; politics-law, which includes our common law background and a commitment to political liberty, individual responsibility, respect for the rule of law, and maintaining the common good; and economic, involving the natural right of private property and a free market economy. The family has been central to each one of these components, as the following examples indicate. Aristotle, perhaps the greatest philosopher, realized that the family had to be the basic unit of society, the first force in the shaping of virtuous individuals and good citizens. There is no doubt about the importance the Judeo-Christian tradition has assigned to the family, viewing it as the primary means for educating, morally shaping, and transmitting religious truths to the next generation. Such key modern political thinkers as Locke and Montesquieu stressed the importance of the family, and America's Founding Fathers viewed it and other social forces as essential for shaping virtue and moral character in the citizenry so that republican government could be sustained. Our common law tradition has accorded a special status and protection to the family, being particularly careful to guard it from arbitrary intrusion and pressures from the state. Aristotle viewed the family as the most basic level of an economy and the primary source of learning about the stewardship of property. Family-owned enterprises have always played a valuable part in the free market economy of the West.

The most pernicious and portentous part of the assault on the traditional notion of the family is that, due to the metaphysical perspective of those carrying it out, it seeks to divorce the family from its spiritual base and from the context of the natural moral order which must govern its activities, those of the individuals making it up, and those of the state in relation to it. When these elements are eliminated, families are weakened and often break apart, and the state comes to view the family as something which exists only at its sufferance to be exploited as it sees fit.

The contributors to this book expose the weaknesses and dangers in the thinking of those taking part — wittingly or unwittingly — in the contemporary assault on the family and parental rights. They provide a much-needed scholarly commentary on this effort as well as an astute, thoughtful, and objective defense of the traditional view of familial and parental rights and responsibilities, including the specific application of this view to public policy on education, abortion and other life issues, juvenile delinquency, and the intervention of state social welfare agencies and the law into the family. Dr. Waters's paper sets the groundwork by discussing the proper ordering of the parent-child relationship as determined by human nature and the natural moral law — behind which stands God — the firmest and surest basis for determining human conduct. He shows how a creeping totalitarian mentality has caused the suppression of parental rights. The short presentations of Mr. Whitehead and Dr. Wolters were originally part of a commentary panel at the symposium on Dr. Waters's paper. They were chosen here because of their particularly insightful elaboration and the additional perspective they present on some of Dr. Waters's key themes. Mr. Whitehead, aware of how parental rights have been suppressed partly in the name of other "rights," discusses the all-important matter of distinguishing true from illusory rights. Dr. Wolters provides an example of the suppression of parental rights by social theorists working in conjunction with government authorities in the area of school desegregation. Mr. Marzen discusses legal developments and court decisions which have in recent years, in contrast to other legal and public policy developments, expanded parental rights, but in *opposition* to the natural moral law Dr. Waters discusses. For example, they have given parents the "right" to end the life of their unborn and defective newborn children. Dr. Rice and Mr. Likoudis both speak about parental rights in the crucial area of education, where they have suffered most grievously in recent decades. Rice focuses mostly on legal developments in the area of parental choice over the manner of education for their children (e.g., types of schools they may attend). Likoudis speaks primarily about how parental rights have been undermined by many programs which have been introduced into school curricula in recent years, such as sex education and values clarification, which have tried to inculcate beliefs and attitudes opposed to the natural moral law. Dr. Rinn speaks about the psychological consequences and general ineffectiveness of so many government programs that have been directed toward helping youth. He gives us an indication of what we are in store for if we let the state take away from parents even more of the prerogative of raising children. Mr. D'Agostino discusses changes in American law in the past generation on matters of parental rights and state intervention into the family, indicating the trends as a growing threat to parents. My paper studies one of these areas of law closely: that relating to child abuse. It shows how laws have frequently been directed against innocent parents and have become a gateway for excessive and unwarranted state intrusion into the family. All the contributors speak about the growth of a dangerous state control in this most intimate aspect of human life — the family — and see its roots in modern secular, statist thought and attitudes. When most Americans seem utterly unaware of such control until they experience the heavy hand of the state in their family life or in that of someone close to them, it is our hope and belief that this book will enlighten them about the gravity of the situation and make at least a small contribution towards correct thinking about the increasingly crucial public issue of parental and family rights.

Stephen M. Krason
Steubenville, Ohio
January 1, 1988

The Basis for the Traditional Rights and Responsibilities of Parents

Raphael T. Waters

The Problem

From the time of Plato's attempt to restructure the political order, there has been no shortage of doctrinal positions concerning the status of the family within that higher society we call the body politic. Plato considered abolishing the former, at least for the guardians and magistrates, when he wrote *The Republic* which degraded women to the inferior position of mere nursemaid.[1]

If some of the Greeks lost sight of the natural order within which a child is best raised, the Romans showed better sense with a higher estimation of family life.[2] Their fidelity to the traditional understanding of the conjugal union, notwithstanding some peculiar defects, must have contributed to the strength of the Empire in no small measure.

In more recent years, however, extreme developments with an anti-family mentality forebode disastrous consequences for

---

[1]Plato, *The Republic*, V, 453 et seq.; Jacques Leclercq, *Marriage and the Family*, 4th rev. ed., trans. T.R. Hanley (New York: Frederick Pustet, 1949), p. 373.

[2]Jacques Leclercq, *ibid.*

the very element from which society is constituted. Acting as buffers between man and the state, mediating institutions such as the family, church, and labor unions have become something modern absolutists cannot tolerate. Hitler, Mussolini, Lenin, and other totalitarians have quickly realized that in order to seize complete authority within the political society, one must have control over family life. They have seen the state — not the family — as the ultimate provider for the needs of a child: his food, his clothing, and above all his education. Civil society reigns supreme in the doctrines of these men, and each citizen is merely a part of the state. He is an individual not a person — at least that is the practical implication. Hence, the citizen is merely a citizen, and his end coincides with the end of the state; his rights, education, and protection all come from that supreme order which owes little allegiance to its members. But man as a person is a whole, having a dignity and end all his own, which places him above the state; for the latter exists ultimately for its members as persons.

Some planners, wishing to assert the primacy of the state, see the parents as standing between its authority and the child.[3] Hence, the readiness to thrust aside the family, allowing parents little decision in the education of their sons and daughters. The basic focus of this paper is the education of children, instead of, more broadly, their rearing. This is in line with St. Thomas Aquinas's saying that education is the key element in childrearing. Also, this is the area in which there has been the greatest threat to parental rights in recent times, although it is getting greater in other areas of childrearing. The state is the agency which grants them security, food, and clothing, they might argue, hence the state is the final arbiter of what they shall learn,

---

[3]Paul Brandwein, *The Social Sciences* (Harcourt, Brace, Jovanovich, 1970) p. T-10 of TE, Level 3 and 4, col. 2, para. 4; Onalee McGraw, *The Family, Feminism and the Therapeutic State* (Washington, DC: The Heritage Foundation, 1980) illustrates many anti-family developments which have taken place in the U.S. in the past decade.

how they shall learn it, and from whom, as well as the values they should accept. A good citizenry under the control and direction of civil authorities, causing no undue economic stress and allowing a fit and healthy race of people, appears more desirable than the production of men who are simply good in keeping with their eternal destiny. In its inordinate pride, the modern state considers itself alone fit to accomplish this task of rearing socially-wise citizens, men and women who will live in peace, not for their own sakes but for the sake of the orderly conducting of affairs under the auspices of the Leviathan, with the parents acting merely as agents of the political authorities.

There appear to be two doctrinal sources for the state's claim to have a direct and immediate right to rear and educate a child: philosophical liberalism and political totalitarianism. It is extraordinary that these two opposing errors should both arrive at a doctrine of educating for the state and not for the sake of the child. Yet, in a way, this is to be expected, for the two extremes ultimately arrive at a common error in their political teaching — loss of freedom for the individual — and, hence, the same might be expected in their educational theory.

Liberalism, anxious to defend the freedom of the individual at all costs, teaches a doctrine of the autonomy of man, seeing in the child one who is directly responsible to the state and not to parents who might influence his development and alienate him from his fellows with divisive results in the political order.[4] The child's freedom of conscience is absolute, it is claimed, so that the state becomes the guardian of that conscience. The interpretation follows of a right to educate which resides immediately and directly in the civil authority. For example:

> The principle was asserted in all its baldness as early as the French Revolution. 'Children belong to the Republic before they belong to their parents,' cried Danton. 'The fatherland,' pontificated Robespierre, 'has the right and

---

[4]Jacques Leclercq, *op. cit.*, pp. 373-375.

duty to rear its children; it cannot commit this trust to family pride or to private prejudices. . . . We want education to be common and equal for all Frenchmen.'. . . According to Saint-Just, 'male children from the age of five to sixteen are raised for the fatherland.'. . . 'The socialist ideal,' wrote Jules Guesde, 'will reduce the family in size to a mother and child during the time of suckling.'[5]

In recent times, some have even seen religious instruction as not only the source of divisiveness among people but also as a source of alienation and mental derangement. Paul Brandwein claims that "Any child who believes in God is mentally ill."[6] It is proposed by Ashley Montagu that "The American family structure produces mentally ill children."[7] It is further alleged that:

> Every child in America who enters school at the age of five is mentally ill, because he comes to school with allegiance toward our institutions, toward the preservation of this form of government we have . . . patriotism, nationalism, sovereignty. . . . All of that proves the children are sick, because the truly well individual is one who has rejected all of those things and is what I would call the true international child of the future.[8]

The sole remedy they propose for this is uniform education to produce unity among the citizenry. Hence, education becomes a mere instrument of social peace and order. The parents are

---

[5]Jacques Leclercq, *op. cit.*, pp. 373-374; cf. Irenaeus Gonzales Moral, *Philosophia Moralis*, (5th ed., Santander, Spain, Editorialis Sal Terrae, 1960, Bibliotheca Comillensis), p. 596, N. 1. 260.

[6]Paul Brandwein, *loc. cit.*

[7]Ashley Montagu, Lecture at Anaheim, California to 1000 home economics teachers, 9th November, 1970: reported in Vince Nesbitt, *Humanistic Morals and Values Education* (Sydney, Australia, 1981), p. 5.

[8]Dr. Pierce of Harvard University, addressing 2000 teachers in Denver, Colorado, 1973. Cited in *Education to Remold the Child*, Parent and Child Advocate, Watertown, Wisconsin, p. 30 according to Vince Nesbitt, *loc. cit.*

seen as mere stand-ins for the state which assumes full authority for the rearing and education of each of its citizens.

The political totalitarians directly claim that all authority is vested in those who govern so that, in keeping with their teaching that man is merely an individual and exists entirely for the state, they demand that education be within the state, by the state, under the direction of the state, and solely for the state.[9] The consciences of the citizens are thus preserved and protected from all other interferences — except that of the state. This is the worst form of socialism for there is no redress. It is the worst form of tyranny for there is no appeal. It is the worst form of slavery for there is no personal master. It is the greatest loss of freedom for there is no escape.

Bucharin, presenting the case for communism, has stated that:

> . . . society possesses an original and fundamental right to the education of children. . . . We must accordingly reject without compromise and brush aside the claim of parents to impart through family education their narrow views to the minds of their offspring . . . the qualifications for educating children are rarer than those needed for bringing them into the world.[10]

The well-known teaching of the Italian Fascists and German National Socialists merely confirm what the Communists have proposed with some modifications.[11]

---

[9]Mehdi Nakosteen, *The History and Philosophy of Education* (New York: The Ronald Press Co., 1965), pp. 574-575; Adolf Hitler, *Mein Kampf* (New York: Reynal and Hitchcock, 1939, complete and unabridged version), pp. 613-636; 692; Benito Mussolini, Speech in the Council of Ministers, 28th March, 1928.

[10]N. Bucharin and E. Preobraschensky, *A.B.C. du Communisme* (Paris, 1923), p. 232, cited in Jacques Leclercq, *op. cit.*, pp. 375-376.

[11]Jacques Leclercq, *ibid.*, pp. 377-378.

The more recent work of Alexander Meiklejohn has shown that the English-Speaking world is not exempt from this statolatry when he says that:

> Education is an expression of the will of some social organism, instinct with one life, moved by one mind. Teacher and pupil . . . are both agents of the state.[12]

From the above can now be seen the radical conflict between opposing attitudes towards the education of man. While from natural law we see clearly that the state exists for man, those who follow the errors of modernity — particularly liberalism and statism — propose that man exists for the state. This extreme and radical opposition cannot be reconciled between the two teachings, only one of which is based in the complex nature of man; the other is based in a doctrine of the denial of the value of man as a person. On the one hand, we have a teaching of the supreme worth of man, and, on the other, the supreme worth of the state with man merely existing as an integral part — an expendable part as recent experience has shown with Nazism, communism, and fascism.

The steady inroads on parental authority pose a grave problem for Western man; examination of the nature of the family and the reproductive process can be a counter to this. For we can discover by reasoning from sound principles that the domestic society occupies a far more important position than the authors cited will allow.

The End as Principle in Practical Matters

In his work on social philosophy which bears the title of *Politics*, Aristotle conveys his understanding of the nature of the

---

[12]Alexander Meiklejohn, *Education Between Two Worlds* (New York, 1942), p. 279, cited in Jacques Maritain, *Education at the Crossroads* (New Haven: Yale U.P., 1943), p. 101.

practical order when he states that, "in actions the final cause is the first principle, as the hypotheses are in mathematics."[13] St. Thomas Aquinas also explains that, "the end . . . is the first principle in all matters of action,"[14] and that, "in things which come to be for the sake of an end, the end holds the same order which the premise holds in demonstrative sciences."[15]

We all recognize that it is not only the individual who functions for some good which he attains as the end of his activities, but also an organization operates equally for an end which is perceived under the character of good. Such a group is known as a moral body and in fact takes its very nature from the end for which it exists. Lacking physical unity, for it is not a stone or a tree or a dog or other bodily thing, the moral body achieves a union of its members through coordinated operation for the sake of an end. This end is known as a good which the individuals have in common, that is, a common good, one which they cannot get alone, otherwise the organization might not be needed. A golf club exists in order to provide recreation for its members who need to share their ability to hit a "pill," chase it, lose it, and then find it. The golf club allows players to share the game for which they have a common love. In like manner, horse-riding clubs, historical associations, and travel-clubs provide the facilities for their members to participate in some good which they can obtain together.

Lying at the foundations of any human organization is the highest of human goods all can share, namely, friendship, which is based on a common love of some good which they seek together within the structure of the moral body which they have formed. That love drives them towards what they desire in common.

---

[13]*Nicomachean Ethics*, VII, c. 8, 1115a, 16.
[14]*Summa Theologica*, I-II, q. 90, a. 1.
[15]*In II Physic.*, lect. 15, n. 273.

The End of the Domestic Society as Principle

The domestic society — no less than any other moral union — exists ultimately for the attainment of an end which demands the cooperation of two human persons. Nature has instituted this small but fundamental group, first of the natural societies and the most basic unit of the state, for the purpose of reproducing the human species. In other words, notwithstanding other ends to be attained in the union, the most ultimate on the human level is the reproduction of the species or production of new, *live* men, the common good of the family.

There are indeed certain other ends of the domestic society, and in recent times, the relative importance of these various ends has been subjected to much scrutiny. But an examination of the physical, physiological and psychological structure of the united pair quickly reveals that the primary concern of *nature* is reproduction.   Some will argue that recreation and not procreation is the end for which genital activity exists; frequently, their intent is to justify the use of contraceptives which, the slightest reflection should inform them, provides the very evidence they need to show that the primary intent of nature is to have a means of reproducing their own kind, for they intend to prevent what nature intends to produce — a child.

A closer analysis reveals that there are two levels within the domestic union, one which we might call the "conjugal society" (husband and wife) and another which we could call the "familial society" (parents and children).[16] It is clear that the former — conjugal society — exists with its own common goods (i.e., goods which husband and wife both share) and individual benefits for

---

[16]Ignatius W. Cox, *Liberty: Its Use and Abuse* (3rd rev. ed., New York: Fordham University Press, 1946), pp. 299-305; Johannes Messner, *Social Ethics: Natural Law in the Western World* (rev., trans. J.J. Doherty, St. Louis: B. Herder, 1965), pp. 397-398; Thomas Higgins, *Man as Man: The Science and Art of Ethics* (rev. ed., Milwaukee: Bruce, 1958), ch. 22-23.

the two persons joined in the conjugal union. If there were not common goods proper to this social level, there would probably be few marriages. For the partners obtain mutual love, mutual aid, and a natural remedy for concupiscence or sexual desire. I am aware that it is common to ridicule this as preparatory for the familial society, the second level within marriage. But nature is hardly so foolish as to introduce disorder into a natural moral body by giving man and woman a strong inclination for each other without some purpose. She does not create problems merely to solve them — or introduce the seeds of stress and disorder unless it fits into some design! For the wedded couple enjoy the fruits of their union as a first step towards a more remote end — reproduction — whereby is introduced another level of the social entity which we commonly know as the family or familial society. It is the purpose of the latter to form a new member of the species.

The terms we use are noteworthy: we speak of "husband and wife" in the case of the conjugal society whereas we speak of a "mother and father" in the case of the familial society. The common sense of the people spontaneously confers these titles in recognition of the function of the persons entering the union. The terms imply the relationships involved: first there is merely the two-way relationship, while in the other case it is obviously threefold.

Now we should be aware that it is impossible to have two primary ends for one being. (This is a metaphysical absurdity since any being has only one form and must have only one end to conform to it.) Every being exists for the sake of its end, and in the case of a moral being, such as the marital union, if there were more than one primary end the existence of the being could be endangered. For "everything guards its unity as it guards its being,"[17] as St. Thomas warns us. Hence, in the marital union, there is subordination of one of the two ends to the other; those

---

[17]*Summa Theologica*, I, q. 11, a. 1.

obtained within the conjugal society are subordinate to that obtained in the familial society. The conjugal society provides the support and means for maintaining the structural integrity, continuity and proper functions of the familial society. In other words, the special developmental climate needed for the due maturation of the offspring is provided by the goods obtained within the conjugal society.

Such a comparison does not lessen the importance of either — but the love, the mutual aid, and the use of the marital right all exist ultimately for the sake of making and developing a new, live man. The whole well-being of the familial society depends very much on the ends obtainable by the couple which exist for the sake of the offspring as well as for their own sake.

This process of reproduction is not completed with the production of the zygote — the minimal physical structure which a new man can have. It is merely the beginning of the undertaking; physical, intellectual, and moral education are necessary to complete the work begun by nature. In addition, it is quite apparent that sustenance is needed during the development of the offspring. We generally term the whole enterprise "the rearing of a child," which can occupy approximately twenty-one years in the life of the family, variable according to the exigencies of the culture, climate, and racial peculiarities.

The understanding of the nature of the domestic society, like that of any other moral organism, demands that we reason from the end as from a principle. From the end, we can see that the family is the necessary productive unit requiring the complementary abilities, personalities, and contributions of both parents so that the child can learn and develop habits and accustomizations, including his artistic skills and moral virtues.

There is a due order established by the nature of man and his needs, whether one be parent or child. It is for this reason that nature has imposed upon the human race that unique contractual union of two people in which the subject is their own bodies; the resulting domestic society is destined to attend to the perfection of both body and soul of their offspring and his generants.

Rights and Duties of Parents

The parents, entering the marital unit with all the privileges appropriate to their state in life, bestow on each other mutual and exclusive rights to the use of the means of reproducing their kind — e.g., rights to each other's bodies — which is precisely what the domestic society is reduced to when stripped of its incidental characteristics. These rights, duly contracted, are so essential to the foundation of civil society that the latter does well to guard jealously their covenant for the contracting parties. This is necessary for the sake of the continuity of the race, not to mention the very existence of civil society itself.

Once these conjugal rights are assumed, there falls on the parents an obligation which their natures and the nature of the domestic society have imposed on them: to accept full responsibility for continuing the process of producing a new man. For since the end is the measure or norm of the activity as well as of the nature of the moral union — i.e., reproduction of the species or the production of offspring — the end being a new LIVE man, the process demands completion. The right to the means imposes on the parents an obligation towards the end in order to conform with the requirements of the natural order — the production of offspring. Parents must finish the work they have begun. This plan or order is both descriptive and preceptive.[18]

Nature does not want a mere embryonic organism. Consequently, the smallest human, known to biologists as the zygote, exists as an intermediate stage of the production of a new

---

[18]Thomas J. Higgins, *op. cit.*, ch. 5, esp. pp. 99-100.

fully-developed organism in keeping with nature's manifest
intention, the production of a new, live man. Hence, it would be
absurd to create embryos, fetuses, or whatever we like to call the
various intermediate stages in the development of new people,
and then to cast them aside. That is precisely what is being done
today by those procuring abortion — failing to meet that
fundamental obligation to sustain and educate. For, since the
end is the measure of the act of generation, the goodness of the
means is derived from the goodness of the end. Therefore, the
goodness of the embryonic man is derived from the goodness of a
complete new member of the human race. If this basic moral
argument could be understood, instead of the secondary
argument from the humanity of the fetus with all the attendant
difficulties it has posed for pro-life protagonists, the discussions
surrounding abortion would have yielded better results in the
great moral dilemma of our confused culture.

Many philosophers leave us with no illusion concerning the
duty which the natural order imposes on man when it is a
question of the reproduction of our species. For example, St.
Thomas makes it clear that:

> Nature does not intend only the generation of offspring, but
> its development and advance right up to the perfect state of
> man forasmuch as he is man, which is the state of virtue.[19]

In similar manner, St. Augustine said:

> As regards the offspring it is provided that they should be
> begotten lovingly and educated religiously.[20]

Again, in his *Ethics*, Aristotle speaks about family life:

---

[19]*Summa Theologica*, Suppl., q. 41, a. 1.
[20]*De Genesi ad litteram*, lib. IX, cap. 7, n. 12.

> Parents have bestowed on their children the greatest benefits in being the cause of their existence, and rearing, and later of their education.[21]

Kant maintains that:

> . . . from the fact of *procreation* in the union . . . there follows the duty of preserving and rearing *children* as the products of this union. Accordingly, children, as persons, have at the same time an original congenital right . . . to be reared by their parents till they are capable of maintaining themselves. . . .[22]

Among modern philosophers, few have been more interested in social matters than John Locke. It is not surprising that he saw the need for family life and its purpose which he defends by saying:

> The power . . . that parents have over their children arises from that duty which is incumbent on them, to take care of their offspring during the imperfect state of childhood.[23]

He continues:

> . . . parents have a sort of rule and jurisdiction over them when they come into the world, and for some time after, but it is but a temporary one.[24]

Consequently, a grave obligation weighs heavily on the parents from the moral point of view. Every social group confers upon its members certain basic rights from which immediately springs a corresponding obligation. But this obligation is the source of further rights since the obligation cannot be met without the possession of rights with respect to other members of the community who, in turn, are obliged to allow the possessors of

---

[21]*Nicomachean Ethics*, VIII, c. 12, 1162a, 5.
[22]*The Science of Right*, First Part, Ch. 2, Sect. III, Title II.
[23]*Concerning Civil Government*, Ch. VI, n. 58.
[24]*Ibid.*, no. 55.

rights to attend to the obligation which is theirs. This is the crux of our question since it is here that the rights of parents arise. For this basic obligation establishes once and for all the rights of which the parents are the subject so that they can complete the task which is their direct responsibility beyond all other claims.[25]

Parents Uniquely Fit to Rear and Educate Their Children

The fittingness of the parents for the job of rearing and educating children can be seen from the fact that nature has endowed them with the proper equipment to embark on a journey lasting all through the diverse stages of physical, intellectual and moral growth in a child. The mutual love of the parents, the aid they can give to each other, and the intimacies they can share, are all a proper climate for the nestling who "gate crashes" with the approval of his Maker(s). What have been called for so long the "secondary ends" of marriage — as if the term secondary were meant to signify inferiority, an utterly false notion — exist to aid in achieving the perfection demanded by the fast-growing organism. The struggle for due completion which every being seeks — for every being loves its own nature by a natural love — is culminated best in family life where there exist two people who love the offspring more than anyone else can, by a deeply-ingrained appetite established in the natures of the parents. The truth of this must be upheld even though some particular parent might reject his own child because of some acquired inclination (i.e., an inclination contrary to his nature) due to a deformity in his personality or other causes (i.e., something caused by temperament or habits). Such an action would be based on the voluntary or arbitrary defiance of nature.

---

[25]Ignatius W. Cox, *op. cit.*, pp. 323-336; Johannes Messner, *op. cit.*, pp. 408-412; St. Thomas Aquinas, *Summa Theologica*, III Suppl., q. 41, a. 1; q. 49, a. 2, ad 1.

The education initiated by the parents in the home; the imparting of values to the child; discussion and acceptance of various family values with the rejection of a great variety of other values; as well as the constant supervision of the application of these values: all of these can only be adequately achieved in practice within the framework of a small society where love and special safeguards protect the younger members. This love emanates best from parents inasmuch as they are most willing to give it to their own offspring since the latter are extensions of their own being.

The development of a child is a rugged and, at the same time, a delicate affair. It is rugged because of the ability of a child to bounce back from setbacks, insults, rebuffs, and other traumatic experiences in life. Yet, at the same time, it is a very delicate process inasmuch as the molding of human character, the unfolding of intellectual and emotional capacities, require special direction within the context of human affection. For those who love him most are best suited to achieve the end demanded by nature since, on account of their special love for the offspring, the parents will automatically seek his good even when it might conflict with their own.

Although matter often impedes the form from attaining the best possible shape and proper size for a species, nature wants physically, psychologically, and morally perfect members of the human race — and so do men, if the recent activities in the medical arts (e.g., genetic engineering, abortion for reasons of fetal deformity) are any criteria — and, therefore, there is no completely satisfactory replacement for the family into which a child is born. His parents love him more than civil society or the state or government could possibly love him. Therefore, they are best fitted to supervise the development of their own offspring right up to its fullest extent according to his nature. In spite of this, the liberals and the state absolutists seem to ignore the fact that "education by the state is education by the functionary, that is to say, by a person who is indifferent."[26]

The child is not the only one educated by the familial society. The parents participate in this process also insofar as they learn and develop as persons benefiting from the familial common good. Nature has marvelously constructed the domestic society so that all persons acquire some benefits from the association. The goods (e.g., love, educatedness, peace and security in the home) are indeed common and to be shared so that the offspring, while proceeding towards full manhood, and undergoing the educative influence, presents himself as a suitable instrument enabling his parents to obtain deeper insights into human nature and its relations with other things.

We return to the term "live man" whereby is signified that each man ought to acquire sufficient science and art to attend to his own welfare. Nature does not want members of the human race who are a burden on the others, men and women who will impede the operation of the body cultural, the body politic, the body economic, or the body recreative, although it should be noted in passing that nature does permit a number of physically or psychologically defective members of the human race. The latter are simply explained as needed in order that greater good might come to the society of men. The great Legislator allows us the means whereby the race might be raised to greater perfection inasmuch as there are a number of us who are born with physical defects and who serve the common good by providing an opportunity to develop the best of human qualities in all of us (e.g., love and sacrifice). In other words, nature allows some imperfections as part of the educative and developmental process.

It becomes clear, then, that the direct right of educating and rearing a child originates in the need to reproduce the species,

---

[26]Jacques Leclercq, *op. cit.*, p. 374, note; cf. Onalee McGraw, *op. cit.*, Ch. 7.

the parents justly claiming educational rights as their proper domain while all attempts at usurping these rights are in conflict with the nature of the domestic society as well as the nature of man — in short, it is against the natural moral law.

It is interesting to note that in Europe when one was either a Catholic or a Jew — and most of Europe was Catholic — St. Thomas argues that:

> . . . it would be an injustice to Jews if their children were to be baptised against their will, since they would lose the rights of parental authority over their children as soon as these were Christians.[27]

St. Thomas justifies the need for this authority when he says that:

> . . . a child is by nature part of its father. Thus, at first, it is not distinct from its parents as to its body, so long as it is enfolded within its mother's womb; and later on after birth, and before it has the use of its free choice, it is enfolded in the care of its parents, which is like a spiritual womb, for so long as a child does not have the use of reason, he does not differ from a non-rational animal. Thus, even as an ox or a horse belongs to someone who according to the civil law, can use them when he likes, as his own instrument, so, according to the natural law, a son, before coming to the use of reason, is under his father's care. Hence, it would be contrary to natural justice, if a child, before coming to the use of reason, were to be taken away from its parent's custody, or anything done to it against its parent's wish.[28]

The very properties of the domestic society, namely, the unity and indissolubility of marriage, are derived from the end intended by nature. Such properties originate in the bond, that is, the form, of the matrimonial unit; for moral bodies have their properties no less than physical bodies. It is the rejection of these properties today which is giving rise to the decay of family life. For the need to perfect the offspring imposes the obligation

[27]*Summa Theologica*, II-II, q. 12, a. 12, sed contra.
[28]*Ibid.*, II-II, q. 10, a. 12, c.

upon the parents. This in turn imposes the two properties inasmuch as the generants, and they alone, permanently united, are best fitted to raise and educate their child. (A permanent union is necessary because if children thought marriage could be dissolved, fear and doubt would destroy their peace of mind.)

Another right, in keeping with the nature of the domestic union and with the essence of man on which that domestic union is founded, is the right to be parents. This springs directly from the very reason for the conjugal union. Parents are united in marriage for the sake of reproduction according to the natural order, and, consequently, their first right in relation to the rest of mankind is to be parents, to reproduce their kind in keeping with a metaphysical principle which describes the appetitive nature of reality, namely: Good is diffusive of itself. The parents, loving the good which they themselves are, have a great urge to diffuse that goodness by producing others like themselves. This urge exists simply because the Supreme Maker of plans has implanted a natural appetite in each thing to attain its own perfection, to guard it, and to reproduce it. This natural appetite is burned into the nature of each being and is the basis of the natural love each parent has for his own child.

The metaphysics of the order within society can be summarized in the following manner:

William
Elizabeth   A 21 year process approximately→   New LIVE man
⬇
Right of sexual congress
⬇
Obligation to perfect the offspring
⬇
Rights with respect to others
⬇
Consequent obligations which others
have to recognize the rights of the parents

Proper Role of the State

From the viewpoint of the state, there is a compelling reason why the rights of parents, and indeed, the obligations on them, ought to be safeguarded. Man is an individual and a person. He is an individual insofar as he is a material entity; he is a person insofar as he has a rational soul and thus exists in his own right, for his own sake and his own personal destiny. As a person, he is a "whole," but as an individual, he is necessarily a part of society — his body makes him indigent. He needs society. The fact that he is in society means that he is part of the state and owes something to it. Thus, insofar as man is an individual, he exists for the state; but insofar as he is a person, the state exists for him (i.e., to help him achieve his end). With this complexity in mind, the place he occupies in society ought to achieve a delicate balance whereby his individuality is suitably developed in the interests of the state, but more importantly, the state ought to demand and protect suitable education, not only for the sake of the political organism but also for the sake of the individual person. No mental gymnastics can justify this unless we fully understand man and the purpose of his existence.

Moreover, the task ought to be carried out by the parents and not the state, for the principle of subsidiarity leaves no room for doubt that the lower functions ought to be performed by lower functionaries since *what can be done by the lower ought not be done by the higher*. The jurisdiction of parents as parents occupies a more restricted functional domain within the framework of civil society. Yet it occupies a prime place according as the latter exists primarily for the sake of the individual person whose educational cradle is the family. The parents are far better qualified to carry on the tasks of every-day living, understanding and tolerating the intimacies and conflicts appropriate to family life; the state, on the other hand, would be better occupied protecting this miniature society rather than attempting to replace it with its own bureaucratic organization.

The family exists for the development of new members of the species while the state exists for family groups containing the new and the older members but must take special care that suitable replacement of its citizens is nurtured within the best possible educational setting. Our human appetites, of which love is principal, come naturally to those whose own offspring are the object of that love and provide the most suitable learning environment.

A consideration of the common goods (i.e., commonly-sought goods) of the family and the state will highlight the legitimacy of the domestic society's claim to be the direct educator of embryonic man. The function of the state is to govern (*Gubernator*, Latin, means to be the helmsman or he who governs or steers). But we might ask: "Govern what?" The most universal social goods are the object of such action. Civil society exists for the attainment of certain common goods such as civic friendship, peace, order, freedom, justice, security, educatedness, and so forth. Desired by every man, woman, and child, these are goods indispensable for a life dedicated to higher things — the matters of the body cultural — for which man has been cast among bodily things. But there is needed a directive or educative and unifying authority to direct us towards those goods, to preserve and protect them, to see that we do not turn from the path leading to them. In other words, the most universal and completely divisible goods (i.e., common goods) are the object of the vision of the civil authorities.

The common good of the domestic society, on the other hand, is nothing other than the new members of the species. This is a good shared and desired by the domestic couple. They have projected a part of themselves into the corporeal world; an extension of each and both of them together, it is indeed a good they seek in common. And it belongs to them and to them alone. Little Joey shares his life with Elizabeth and William and not with others. This is different from the civil society where the common goods, the civic common goods (e.g., peace, order, and other nonmaterial goods), are divisible and to be sought by all who wish to join civil society.

The position of a civil authority in society is primarily one of a *special* educator.[29] Its capacity as supervisor demands that it advise its citizens to nurture the common good largely by urging that it be cultivated and not harmed in any way. A healthy attitude towards the common good is itself a common good; the more we have of it, the more each person benefits as with any of the common goods, since they exist for the good of the state and for the good of the individual members of the state. As beneficiaries, the latter ought to be good men, the best kind of citizens. Good men will be good citizens but good citizens might not be good men.[30] The due perfection of the person will carry a large bonus for civil society, hence protection of the family unit is in the best interest of the state (e.g., in preventing juvenile delinquency).

Totalitarian Mentality

The principal threat to the authority of parents can come from civil authority inasmuch as some theorists, in their assaults on the family, intend that the supreme social body assume the rights of parenthood. Hence, the need to reinforce our understanding of the very source of parental authority, the fountainhead of the jurisdiction of those who generate the offspring, in order that we might avoid making the kind of mistake so well noted by Aristotle when he saw that a small error in principle leads to a great error in the conclusion.[31]

The many advocates for the right of the political authority to take over in an absolute way the education of children are

---

[29]John Thornhill, *The Person and the Group* (Milwaukee: Bruce, 1967), pp. 176-180.

[30]Aristotle, *Politics*, III, c. 4, 1276b, 34-35; VII, c. 14, 1333a, 12-17.

[31]*Nicomachean Ethics*, I, c. 7, 1098b, 5-6.

motivated by a totalitarian mentality. According to these planners, the state is the end of man and not the means whereby man obtains his happiness.[32] The state, then, becomes the only person, the possessor of rights and their sole source. It certainly has an indirect claim whereby the governing authority can ensure that there is no neglect of the educational rights of the child but does not have a direct and immediate right to assume full parental authority. The parents are not morally free to become mediate educators, acting on behalf of the state — even if they decided to be. Children are members of civil society but only by the mediacy of the family, which itself is prior to the state, as Aristotle shows when he says that "man in his nature is much more conjugal than political, inasmuch as the family is an earlier and more fundamental institution than the state."[33]

It might be argued that each person is ultimately a citizen of the political society and hence the latter stands to benefit from good citizenship or suffer from a defect thereof. Therefore, it is sometimes concluded, the state has a prior right to raise and educate its citizens, and, consequently, the parents have merely a delegated right, acting on behalf of the government. This objection can spring from a false understanding of the nature of man. As a person, as well as an individual, man is not merely a part of society but also exists for his own sake, not merely for the state as his end. He thus deserves education — being developed for his own sake — not mere training — being developed for the sake of the state. State absolutism denies man's personality in favor of his individuality and requires his complete submersion within the body politic. This can only result in a loss of freedom and consequent unhappiness.

Speaking of a community of wives and children as envisaged in *The Republic* of Plato, Aristotle criticized the resultant neglect which is inevitable when he said: "Everybody is more inclined to

---

[32]See note 5 above.
[33]*Nicomachean Ethics*, VIII, c. 12, 1162a, 16-18.

neglect the duty which he expects another to fulfill."[34] The Philosopher saw that education applied to commonly-owned sons would occasion a neglect of their intellectual development. He gave as reason that, "Everyone thinks chiefly of his own, hardly at all of the common interest."[35] How carefully would the state educate the sons and daughters except for its own sake and not for the sake of the sons and daughters themselves? Who could be sure that the state will educate properly — i.e., educate for the educated — when so many advocate that the object of education is to produce good citizens in order to obtain an orderly society among men (i.e., the state educating for its own purpose)? Moreover, we can be reasonably certain that many citizens would be inclined to leave the educational burden to the state. Indeed, is this not what is being done now? Is there not within the contemporary society the supposition that education is best left to schools?

In the same manner, *licensing* parents either to have children or to be educators of their own children flies directly in the face of the natural order. Onalee McGraw reports that licensing has been seriously proposed by a "high ranking HEW official, Eddie Bernice Johnson . . . at a Child Abuse Conference in Dallas."[36] Johnson stated the following:

> We require almost every endeavor or profession to be licensed — why not the single most important responsibility which a parent can ever have?[37]

Johnson contended that licensing people to become parents would enable society:

---

[34]*Politics*, II, c. 3, 1261b, 36.
[35]*Ibid.*, 34.
[36]Cited by Onalee McGraw, *op. cit.*, p. 41.
[37]*Ibid.*

to be secured by a knowledge of parenting skills and techniques which allow the family to have some background concerning how to parent.[38]

At the outset, this implies an unwarranted superiority of the state. The state completes the family in the arrangement of natural things but there is a natural priority in the domestic society whereby the latter can justly claim to be the hearth of the human heart. At the mother's knee, small hearts, tiny minds, and fragile limbs all learn how to become strong, supple, and toughened against the assaults of life. No statesman has enough love to go around to so many little bodies and souls, nor can he be trusted enough to sacrifice himself for the good of Joey, Betty and Tommy. His love is usually for mankind!

The priority of the parents in matters of education did not go unnoticed by the General Assembly of the United Nations on December 10, 1948 when it was agreed that, "Parents have the prior right to choose the kind of education that shall be given to their children."[39] This was confirmed at the Congress of the International Union for Freedom in Education, held at Bruges, Belgium, in 1953 when it was proclaimed that:

> The parent's right to complete freedom in choosing to have their children educated according to their religious and philosophical convictions is asserted in the United Nations universal declaration of human rights.
>
> The right of parents to complete freedom in choosing the education of their children is not an empty liberty to bear the cost of sending their children to private or parochial schools. It is one that involves the corresponding duty in strict justice on the political authorities of each nation to furnish parents the financial assistance necessary to exercise the right.

---

[38]*Ibid.*
[39]*The Universal Declaration of Human Rights*, Article 26, 3.

This direct right of parents to sustain and educate their own offspring in no way conflicts with their right — indeed, it can become a grave obligation for some — to delegate their authority to others inasmuch as the parents themselves do not have the ability to develop all the requisite habits and skills in their own child. This can be easily seen in the various scientific, linguistic, moral, and literary domains which demand the activity of those who have properly mastered their discipline.

Conclusion

It is clear that parents have authority over their own offspring. There is little chance that other private members of society will want to assume this authority, but there is a real reason to fear the assumption of parental rights by the state. It is equally clear that this assumption would run counter to the best interests of the child and, ultimately, of the state.

The incursions of the political authorities, the drive by secular humanists and so-called sex-educators, as well as some recent decisions of the Supreme Court of the United States, such as those on abortion, all run counter to the order established by nature. Discovery of the order natural to the family and natural to civil society depends on a prior discovery of the nature of man and its essential properties. We are morally free about many things associated with the social order; for example, we are free about who we will marry, which society we shall live in, and who will govern our societies, as well as a host of other things. But there are other matters about which we are not morally free, and these have to be determined by an adequate study of the nature of man followed by an adequate study of the nature of each of the social bodies: the domestic and political societies most notably.

Those who wish to impose an order based on the arbitrary decision of some minority, or even of some majority, threaten the peace and freedom of every member of civil society. Above all, under such a social order, a few might temporarily find human happiness, but most members would discover what earlier civilizations found to their great regret, namely, that to live counter to that order best established by nature alone involves enormous cost in human terms.

The enemies of the domestic society demand conformity whereby each person becomes an individual citizen existing solely for the sake of the welfare of the political group to which the family belongs. Although these enemies see the domestic unit standing in their way, human offspring need the family. They ought to be reared with a love of the goods most fitting to their natures as persons since, as such, they have a value of their own and not as mere individuals disposable for the good of the social whole.

Of what does education of the young consist? It is movement towards the acquisition of the intellectual and moral virtues so that the child may become all that he ought to be and capable of all that he ought to do.[40] The parents alone are sufficient guardians of this for their own child. Therefore, they alone have inalienable rights to develop that child to the perfection of full humanity.

---

[40]Pius XI, *Divini Illius Magistri* (Christian Education of Youth), "Importance of Christian Education."

Rights, Real and Ersatz

Kenneth D. Whitehead

Professor Waters has given us a classic statement of the philosophical basis for the rights and responsibilities of parents. It is also a *true* statement, grounded in a view of the nature of man, of the family, and of society which is derived in turn from a philosophy of nature which is at one and the same time that of the *philosophia perennis* and that of the common sense of the average man. Both the common sense of the average man and the *philosophia perennis* hold that what exists out there in the world is real, can be known, and usually has some discernible purpose — as eyes exist in order to enable us to see, for example. It is not possible to establish "rights" that are truly rights on any other basis; unless they are grounded in reality, they are nothing except what somebody happens to assert they are.

Common sense revolts against such a conclusion. It is almost impossible to find anyone who doubts that *he* has rights, for example; nor is it common for any of the diverse groups which make up society ever to fail to assert their rights. The all-important philosophical question becomes, however, what these rights are actually based on; their grounding in reality is the key to whether they are actually rights or not.

Our Republic, of course, was founded on the basis of human rights. The Declaration of Independence speaks of everybody's right to "life, liberty, and the pursuit of happiness." The Constitution speaks, more precisely, of rights to "life, liberty, and property." The latter are rights we may not be deprived of without due process of law under the Constitution. Our Republic was founded on the presumed objective existence of all these rights, a far cry from "oriental despotism."

As Gideon said in the Bible, however, "If the Lord be with us, then why has all this befallen us?" Never have we heard more rhetoric about rights emanating from so many different sources than is the case today. Yet, at the same time, some of these same rights formerly assumed to be fundamental are casually put aside as if they did not exist. This society of ours based on the presumed existence of rights grounded in the nature of things now routinely denies the most basic right of all — the right to life — to a million or more unborn children each year. This has become possible due to a decision of the U.S. Supreme Court establishing a so-called right to privacy which supposedly entitles a woman to do away at will with the child inside her womb. The right to life mentioned in both the Declaration of Independence and the Constitution has suddenly been replaced by a right to privacy mentioned in neither.

What has happened to the very concept of rights in a topsy-turvy situation such as this? What has happened is that the relentless march of positivism and existentialism and Marxism and the like has succeeded in cutting the formerly solid ground out from under the very idea that there are objective rights that inhere in the nature of human beings, in other words, that there are rights that human beings enjoy by virtue of the fact that they are human beings. According to the philosophies fashionably accepted today, neither man nor the family nor society has any fixed nature. Consequently, no fixed rights can be predicated of man, the family, or society. The only rights they might possibly have would be those which, at some point, they might possibly be *asserted* to have. Under this system, the rights they might end up with in practice would be only those most loudly or insistently asserted and repeated, that is to say, those enforced by some sort of *power*. In a world no longer anchored in objective reality but moved instead by subjective will, might does, in fact, make right.

Indeed, the relationship between certain fashionable modern philosophical views and the modern totalitarian state is a well-established one. One thinks of George Orwell's novel *1984*. We can see how true Orwell's prophecies were. Although the tyrannies he predicted have not befallen us in exactly the way (or in the degree) that he imagined in his novel, the kind of totalitarian thinking he described appears all too often in the contemporary world: "War is peace, freedom is slavery, ignorance is strength." From where the modern world is unsteadily attempting to stand, philosophically speaking, we can all too easily fall into the totalitarian solutions Orwell feared and described. Occasionally, we do: whole classes, such as the unborn, are currently disenfranchised. It is only a step to the disenfranchisement of the old, the defective, the incurably ill — Adolph Hitler's "useless eaters."

Contempt for truth, for reality, for what really is out there is the essence of the modern totalitarian idea. Hannah Arendt made this clear more than thirty-five years ago in her great study *The Origins of Totalitarianism* when she remarked that the Soviet Communist claim that the Moscow subway was the first in the world simply meant that the Communists had not yet reached Paris in order to *make* their claim true by destroying the Paris subway. The aim of totalitarianism is to remake reality, and, in the field of human rights, we have recently seen this remaking process at work with a vengeance. Real, objective rights of persons, grounded in the nature of things, are denied and trampled upon as in the cases of those classes we have named: the unborn, the defective, etc. At the same time, a whole new range of ersatz rights are proclaimed, "rights" which, in most cases, simply serve to erode further the real rights of children, parents, families — indeed, of all of us. For instance:

— Spouses are now asserted to have the equal and unilateral "right" to cancel their marriage vows (presumably in the interests of "the pursuit of happiness").

— Women, according to the Supreme Court, now legally
enjoy the right of privacy which enables them to have their
living, though unborn, children aborted.

— Parents of defective children have now been authorized
by lower courts to allow these children to be starved to
death — this is another new "right" of these parents.

— Children are now said by advocacy groups to have the
right to escape from parental authority and control in
matters of sex and the like, and courts have upheld these
new "rights." Minor girls are held by the courts, for
example, to have the right to be provided contraception and
abortion services without parental knowledge or consent.

— Everybody, according to a popular school of thought,
now has the right to die "with dignity" — at their own option,
of course. This "right to die" will shortly — and logically —
entail a "right to kill" those who ought to be electing their
option to die but do not. This has already happened with
the severely disabled.

These are just a few of the strange new "rights" that have
been emerging in the past few years. And, of course, when they
do emerge they already have about them the quality of
inevitability. We have almost reached the point already where
practically anything can now be asserted as a right and be taken
seriously. Tenants now presumably enjoy the same right not to
pay their rent that landlords have to let their property
deteriorate.

We must take note of the fact that the new rights being
asserted in place of the old natural rights rarely, if ever, have
corresponding obligations that accompany them. With reference
to our topic, Professor Waters speaks of "conjugal rights" creating
"an obligation on the parents . . . to accept full responsibility for
continuing the process of producing a new man." This idea of
rights being linked up with obligations is true of the real rights
grounded in the nature of things, but it is not true of the novel
ersatz rights which we have been considering.

Where can we find a way out of our dilemma? Obviously, the way out has to be a revival of the kind of concept of true rights and obligations set forth in Professor Waters's paper — a concept of rights and obligations based solidly on the nature of things and upon what is true. Only then can we affirm properly the traditional rights and responsibilities of parents. We must strive to bridge the gap between the kind of analysis Professor Waters has provided and the typical kind of non-thinking that unfortunately passes for today's conception of human rights. A continuation of rational, civil discourse is imperative. After all, as Professor Waters has pointed out, man does, in fact, have a rational nature that predisposes him to assent to conclusions reached by rational means. This is a basic truth and is part of the nature of things, just as fundamental human rights are, whether or not they are denied or distorted. We must, therefore, patiently try to continue to make the kind of case that Professor Waters has made here even in the face of the discouragement that is all too likely to afflict us in the present climate.

School Desegregation Policy: State Disregard of the Rights of Black and White Parents

Raymond D. Wolters

I reach some of the same conclusions as the other contributors on the basis of my own observations as an historian of the recent American experience. I have noted especially in the last decade or so that there has been a great deal of talk about "children's rights" and less talk about parental rights. Some of the most influential advocates of children's rights begin with observations that some parents are not protecting their children. Then they use instances of child abuse to justify a general transfer of authority from the parents to social workers and lawyers. Believing that child abuse is not unusual, the advocates of children's rights maintain, if I may quote one of them, Howard Cohen, "We must be ready to accept the idea that dealing with child abuse will mean changing the structure of all relationships between adults and children, not merely the bad ones." Since we cannot say in advance which adults are likely to abuse their children and which are not, again quoting Cohen, "we have to find a way to build checks against child abuse in all our relationships with children." Cohen is not alone in thinking there is not only child abuse but systematic mistreatment of children.

Kenneth Kenniston has said, "In spite of our tender sentiments we really do not like children. We are interested only in shaping and controlling their lives." Walter Mondale has said, "It is a national myth that we love our children." Since they see the family as a combat zone, many advocates of children's rights maintain that children should be given legal rights that they can enforce against their parents. They say that children should have a right to adequate nutrition, free health care, birth control information, and, of course, legal counsel. The only adults some children should trust are not their parents but social workers and lawyers.

Professor Waters, on the other hand, has shown that traditional parental rights are deeply rooted in Aristotelian and Thomistic philosophy. Others have criticized the children's rights advocates for proposing a solution out of proportion to the problem it addresses — a sort of wholesale solution to a retail problem.

My colleague at the University of Delaware, Jan Blits, has said that the worst situations are not the normal experience and do not justify a radical change in approach to the American family. In my own writing on race relations, and most recently on desegregation law, I have focused on what I consider the rather arrogant elitism of many of the reformers. In the landmark legal case on desegregation, *Brown v. Topeka Board of Education*, back in 1954, the Supreme Court ordered local authorities to establish racially non-discriminatory school systems. Fourteen years later, in *Green v. New Kent County*, the Court also prohibited racially neutral assignments that did not lead to racially balanced enrollments.

Let me explain. New Kent County is situated in Virginia about half way between Williamsburg and Richmond. It is a rural county which in 1968 had about 1300 students altogether. Seven hundred forty of them were black. Each of the schools was a combined elementary and high school, and, prior to *Brown*, the schools had been racially segregated with all the blacks attending the George Watkins School on the west side of the county and all the whites attending the New Kent School on the eastern side of the county. Until 1965, Watkins remained all black and New Kent remained all white. Then, to continue receiving money after passage of the 1964 Civil Rights Act, school authorities adopted a plan that gave students free transportation to whichever school they wished to attend. Thirty-five black students chose to attend New Kent School in 1965. The number increased to 111 in 1966 and 115 in 1967; but no white student ever chose to enroll in Watkins. The black plaintiffs and their NAACP attorneys conceded in the litigation before the Supreme Court that their choice had been completely free and unrestricted. They conceded that no pressures of any sort had been exerted. The Supreme Court, nevertheless, decided that New Kent County had not established a racially non-discriminatory school system. Since one school was still 100% black and the other 80% white, the courts said that black parents were somehow given to understand that their children should continue to enroll in the old colored school, Watkins. In the oral argument before the Supreme Court, Chief Justice Warren said, "Social and cultural influences in New Kent were such that it made it impossible for black parents to choose freely." Justice Marshall had to be reminded twice that the black plaintiffs had conceded that their choice was free and unrestricted. By putting the words "freedom of choice" in quotation marks in the opinion that he drafted for the Supreme Court, Justice William Brennan implied that blacks could not make a truly free choice of schools.

Now this *Green* case is not as well known as *Brown*, but it is every bit as important, I believe. It prepared the way for racial quotas and busing for racial balance. The point I wish to stress is that in New Kent County there was no evidence of child abuse. This was not a case where the court was stepping in to protect children from the occasional, all too frequent, forms of child abuse. Instead, the Justices simply assumed that black parents were incapable of choosing wisely for their children.

I would suggest, then, that policies of assigning children to schools on the basis of race in order to promote what the state considers the "proper amount of mixing," is another example of denial of traditional parental rights. The autonomy of the family is involved here. One U.S. Senator has said, "Just as the parent determines what he wants for his child, so do the multitudes of parents who group themselves together in neighborhoods and communities have the right to determine what kind of culture will be the setting for the education of their children." Another Senator said something similar, "Many parents make extreme sacrifices to provide a particular learning environment for their children. For them, the purpose of education goes beyond simple intellectual development and extends to shaping the character and values of the next generation."

Because of differentials in academic achievement, many middle class parents are opposed to proportional mixing. With rates of drug use, early pregnancy, and illegitimacy climbing in middle class communities, many concerned parents wish above all to separate their children from the pull of downward mobility. I think this is every bit as true of middle class black parents as it is of middle class whites. They understand the influence of the peer group and consider it an unwarranted intrusion if the state insists on exposing their children to the underclass. Despite the reassurances of liberal sociologists, many parents are convinced that their children will not benefit from that sort of mixing.

It seems to me that the question of parental rights is very much a live issue today. It is put before us not only in the philosophical sense but by some of the major social policies which the nation has confronted.

Parental Rights and the Life Issues

Thomas J. Marzen

It has long been acknowledged that parents have a fundamental right under the United States Constitution to the care, custody, and control of their minor children.[1] More recently, courts have held that there exist other fundamental rights — in particular, a "right to abortion"[2] and a "right to die"[3] — that introduce new, disturbing themes into developing case law on the scope and nature of parental prerogatives under the Constitution.

To what extent do the parents of a minor daughter have a protectable right to consent to or have notice of her proposed abortion? Does the father of an unborn child have any protectable right to prevent the destruction of his offspring, or at least to know that his child is about to be aborted? Do parents have a right to withhold life-saving medical treatment, nutrition, or hydration from their child born with a disability?

The courts have, to greater or lesser degrees, attempted to explore and to answer such questions. The nature of their often contradictory replies and incomplete inquiries may have

---

[1]See *Wisconsin v. Yoder*, 406 U.S. 205 (1972); see also *Id.* at 232-34 [citing *Pierce v. Society of Sisters*, 268 U.S. 510 (1925); *Prince v. Massachusetts*, 321 U.S. 158 (1944); *Meyer v. Nebraska*, 262 U.S. 390 (1923)].

[2]*Roe v. Wade*, 410 U.S. 113 (1973).

[3]See e.g., *In re Quinlan*, 70 N.J. 10, 355 A.2d 647, *cert. denied*, 429 U.S. 922 (1976).

significant consequences for the legal future of parental rights and interests, as well as for the right to life explicitly acknowledged by the Fourteenth Amendment to the U.S. Constitution.

Moreover, the manner in which these legal issues have been framed may have a substantial impact on policy questions raised by developing medical technology — questions raised by such matters as surrogate parenting, out-of-body fertilization techniques, and, at the other end of the life cycle, by active and passive euthanasia of incompetent and seriously ill individuals.

Parenting necessarily involves the creation and nurture of a new human being, so it is inevitable that an inquiry into the nature and scope of parental rights would involve some exploration of the degree of responsibility and authority that parents have — or should have — for the very life of their child. Yet, if our law acknowledges that parents have very broad power over the care of their child, it has never been acknowledged in the Anglo-American legal tradition that parents have any "right" to deprive their child of life or of the necessities of life.[4] Even when the legal fiction that children were mere chattel of parents — especially the father — persisted, the Anglo-American legal tradition, unlike some ancient and primitive cultures,[5] never countenanced infanticide by parents. Our criminal law has punished and continues to punish infanticide as homicide, pure and simple, notwithstanding the parental status of the perpetrator.

---

[4]Robertson, *Involuntary Euthanasia of Defective Newborns: A Legal Analysis*, 27 *Stan. L. Rev.* 213, 219-22 (1975).

[5]See generally Bopp & Balch, "The Child Abuse Amendments of 1984 and Their Implementing Regulations: A Summary," 1 *Issues L. & Med.* 91 (1985); Moseley, "The History of Infanticide in Western Society," 1 *Issues L. & Med.* 345 (1986); Williamson, "Infanticide: An Anthropological Analysis," in *Infanticide and the Value of Life* (M. Kohl ed. 1978); M. Piers, *Infanticide: Past and Present* (1978).

American law has discarded the concept of parental possession of the child as property; it has considerably expanded the authority of the State to interfere in the family system in order to protect the supposed interests of children. Whether or not such state intervention is always desirable or defensible, it is plainly warranted by the various Juvenile Court Acts and child-neglect statutes in every state when the life of the child is placed in jeopardy by parental neglect or abuse.[6] No jurisdiction lets parental child abuse, much less child killing, go unpunished. Failure to provide the necessities of life — food, water, shelter, and necessary medical care — is never warranted, except when it is simply impossible to provide them.

Whatever the scope or nature of the parental right to the care and custody of children, therefore, it does not encompass a right to deny the child of life or of the necessities of life. Such conduct is not protected in our legal tradition and is surely not fundamental to our concept of ordered liberty, criteria necessary to recognition of the existence of a constitutionally protectable right.[7]

This limitation on the scope of parental rights is logical and comports with the explicit priorities established by the Constitution. Whatever parental right might be asserted, it cannot supervene a right to continued existence. Life is a prerequisite to the assertion of any personal right, including parental rights, and must thus be given priority in any comparative balance. Moreover, although parental rights were no doubt deemed implicit in the order of things on which the Framers of the Constitution built, they were nowhere mentioned. On the other hand, a "right to life" is explicitly acknowledged by the Constitution to all persons and citizens, including infants and children.[8] Rights that derive from the plain language of the

---

[6]Robertson, *supra* note 4, at 222-27.

[7]*Palko v. Connecticut*, 302 U.S. 319, 325 (1937).

[8]U.S. Const. amend XIV, section 1, "No state shall . . . deprive any person of life, liberty, or property without due process of law. . . ."

constitution should not be supervened by rights derived through inference or implication.

Although there are inevitable difficulties in complex circumstances, few would now question this general principle: that the life of a child takes precedence over asserted parental rights and interests. When applied either to abortion or to instances in which life-preserving treatment is denied to a newborn child, this principle would plainly indicate that parents cannot properly assert any "right" that encompasses conduct or negligence that results in the death of their child, born or unborn.

Near universal acceptance of this rule makes it necessary to assert that a child is not fully human — in effect, not really a human child at all — in order to justify conduct that would result in the child's death. Thus, in order to justify abortion, it is first necessary to deny that an *unborn* child is the proper subject of a right to life on account of the undeveloped biological status of the child or the location of the child within the womb. In order to justify denial of non-futile life-saving treatment or sustenance to a disabled newborn that would be provided to other children, it is first necessary to suppose that the value of such a child's life is diminished. In either case, the human nature of the child is denied in order to warrant parental decisions to deprive the child of life. The human fetus and retarded neonate are deemed so significantly different from other human beings that they can receive radically different treatment. Otherwise, it would be logically necessary to admit that parents may also deprive, for example, a perfectly healthy three year old child of life in the same fashion and for the same reasons that abortion is performed or that nutrition or treatment is denied to a disabled child — a conclusion that almost no one would concede.

This tendency to devalue the life of the unborn or disabled child thus underscores a fundamental mental premise of our legal tradition and social consensus: that any asserted parental "right" to bring about the death of a child is no right at all. Whatever the scope of the parental right to the care, custody, and control of a minor child, it is not broad enough to encompass conduct or negligence that would cause the child's death.

This conclusion warrants special emphasis because one way to view developing case law on abortion and infanticide is as representing an extension of parental rights beyond their legitimate bounds. Both the parental "right to privacy" that includes abortion and the supposed right of parents to withhold treatment and care from disabled newborns are ostensibly rooted in an overly broad concept of parental rights that has been developed to apply to these special cases. This judicial deference to the newly recognized "parental right" to abort and to make life-denying treatment decisions, when placed alongside judicial hostility to far more traditionally entrenched parental prerogatives, strongly implies that reliance on this expanded concept of parental rights in these contexts is merely a pretext to justify an underlying hostile judgment about the human value of unborn and disabled children. It conceals a judicial policy preference in favor of wide-spread abortion and against the survival of disabled infants, rather than displaying a time preference in favor of parental prerogatives.

Judicial Origins

When the Supreme Court held that there exists a right of privacy broad enough to encompass the decision to abort, it cited a number of previous decisions that together, the Court believed, formed a Constitutional "penumbra" that protected abortion practices from state interference.[9] Components of this constitutional patchwork were assembled from decisions relating to the First, Fourth, Fifth, Ninth, and Fourteenth Amendments to the Constitution, but the Court traced its decision recognizing a

---

[9]*Roe v. Wade*, 410 U.S. at 152.

right to abortion most directly to the "Fourteenth Amendment's concept of personal liberty and restrictions on state action."[10]

The case cited in support of the Fourteenth Amendment as the principal progenitor of this "right of privacy" was *Meyer v. Nebraska*,[11] where the Court held in 1923 that the State could not constitutionally interfere with parental decisions to educate children in a foreign language, striking down a World War I Nebraska statute that made instruction in the German language a crime. The Court also cited *Pierce v. Society of Sisters*,[12] a 1925 decision in which an Oregon law banning religious instruction of children was held unconstitutional in similar deference to parental prerogatives, as well as several other cases relating to family matters.[13] Cases recognizing a constitutionally protected parental right to care and custody of children under the Fourteenth Amendment were therefore also conceived to form a principle basis for the right to abortion: the right of the parent to educate the child was thought directly analogous to the right to abortion. Indeed, the Court, in *Maher v. Roe*,[14] later relied on an extended analogy to the parental rights cases to decide whether the State was compelled to fund abortion if it funded other medical procedures. In essence, the Court held that the State need not fund a parental decision to abort any more than it has to fund a parental decision to educate a child in a foreign language or in a religious school.[15]

The analogy drawn by the Court between parental rights and the abortion right is rooted in the conceptual nature of the right of privacy, as opposed to more affirmative individual rights.

---

[10]*Id.* at 153.

[11]*Id.* at 152 (citing *Meyer*, 262 U.S. at 399).

[12]*Id.* at 153 (citing *Society of Sisters*, 286 U.S. at 535).

[13]*Id.* at 152-53 [citing *Prince*, 321 U.S. at 166; *Loving v. Virginia*, 388 U.S. 1, 12 (1967); *Skinner v. Oklahoma*, 316 U.S. 535, 541-42 (1942); *Eisenstadt v. Baird*, 405 U.S. 438, 454 (1972)].

[14]432 U.S. 464 (1977).

[15]*Id.* at 476-77.

In addition to the parental rights cases, the *Roe* Court also cited, in support of the proposition that there exists a right to abortion, Fourth Amendment search and seizure cases that related to the individual's right to be free of bodily intrusion — a right to possess and control one's body.[16] Yet bodily autonomy was specifically rejected by the Court as a basis for its decision recognizing the abortion right. As the Court stated in *Roe*:

> It is not clear to us that the claim asserted by some amici that one has an unlimited right to do with one's body as one pleases bears a close relationship to the right of privacy previously articulated in the Court's decisions.[17]

Instead, the Court described the nature of the right if found as a "zone of privacy" formed by the woman and her physician that protected their mutual decision. This right to privacy does not attach to the woman alone, but to the physician-patient *relationship* — with the physician as the final arbiter. In explaining this conception, the Court stated that:

> [*Roe v. Wade*] vindicates the right of the physician to administer medical treatment according to his professional judgment up to the points where important state interests provide compelling justifications for intervention. Up to those points, the abortion decision in all its aspects is inherently, and primarily, a medical decision, and basic responsibility for it must rest with the physician.[18]

Indeed, in *Connecticut v. Menillo*,[19] which involved a challenge to a requirement that physicians perform abortion, the Court later

---

[16]*Roe v. Wade*, 410 U.S. at 152 [citing *Terry v. Ohio*, 392 U.S. 1, 8-9 (1968); *Katz v. United States*, 389 U.S. 347, 350 (1967); *Body v. United States*, 116 U.S. 616 (1886)].

[17]*Id.* at 153.

[18]*Id.* at 165-66.

[19]423 U.S. 9 (1975).

held, in effect, that there exists no right to abortion without the presence of a physician.[20]

The Court's decision in *Roe*, therefore, claims direct conceptual heritage not from the "bodily autonomy" cases, but from those cases it cited that recognize the existence of fundamental rights that attach to what one commentator has called "relational interests."[21] The woman-physician relationship, at least when it concerns reproductive matters, was understood to be directly analogous to parent-child and spousal relationships and to warrant constitutional protection that is at least as strong — never mind that the physician-patient relationship has hardly been otherwise regarded as sacrosanct by the law either in tradition or in present practice.

Justice Stewart, although he voted in favor of *Roe*, was plainly unhappy with this formulation of the abortion right, and he carried on a minor campaign to recast it as an individual right in the nature of a right to bodily autonomy. He flatly refused to employ the physician-woman zone of privacy concept and, when he wrote the majority opinion in *Harris v. McRae*,[22] referred exclusively to a "right to choose" abortion. With his departure from the Court, however, the relational privacy basis for the abortional liberty is now unchallenged. It plainly triumphed, and in the Court's most recent decisions, in *Akron v. Akron Reproductive Health Services*,[23] *Planned Parenthood Ass'n v. Ashcroft*,[24] and *Thornburgh v. American College of Obstetricians & Gynecologists*.[25]

What information the State can seek to assure the woman prior to abortion was deemed to be a matter for physician

---

[20]*Id.* at 11.
[21]Green, *Relational Interests*, 29 *Ill. L. Rev.* 460 (1934).
[22]448 U.S. 297 (1980).
[23]462 U.S. 416 (1983).
[24]462 U.S. 476 (1983).
[25]476 U.S. 747 (1986).

discretion.[26] The safety standards for the woman during abortion, including whether abortion would or should be performed in hospitals during the second trimester of pregnancy, were deemed to be matters determined by "accepted medical practice."[27] If the abortion right had been conceived as a simple individual "right to choose," then such levels of deference to physician discretion would not logically have been warranted. That it continued to be understood as a right that attaches to the physician-woman relationship strongly reinforces the analogy to the parent-child relationship. Physicians were deemed constitutionally privileged to withhold or to relate information on such matters as fetal development as they see fit, and to perform abortion in accord with whatever standards are accepted by their fellow abortion practitioners — much as parents can educate children and choose their life styles and circumstances with a wide degree of constitutional latitude. "Doctor knows best" has been raised to the constitutional stature that "father knows best" once had in popular culture.

The same influence of the parent-child analogy can be seen in developing case law on infanticide, euthanasia, and the "right to die."

The first and most important modern case relating to these matters, *In re Quinlan*,[28] specifically held that there exists a right to die — at least for the terminally ill and for the permanently comatose or vegetative[29] — that is an aspect of the right of privacy.[30] When the individuals who are the beneficiaries of this right to die are incompetent — which is the usual case in which a legal controversy will arise — this "right" can be imputed by way of substituted judgment to a third party to be exercised on behalf

---

[26]*Akron*, 462 U.S. at 443; *Thornburgh*, 476 U.S. at 759-65.
[27]*Akron*, 462 U.S. at 434-39.
[28]70 N.J. 10, 355 A.2d 647, *cert. denied*, 429 U.S. 922 (1976).
[29]*Id.* at 9-14, 355 A.2d at 662-64.
[30]*Id.* at 11, 355 A.2d at 663.

of the incompetent individual.[31] The "right" traded-off is fundamental in nature, so that the legal fiction of substituted judgment becomes the sole vehicle in our law by which a constitutional right is fully transferred from one person to another. The result is that the legal fiction of substituted judgment becomes the sole vehicle in our law by which a constitutional right is fully transferred from one person to another. The result is that decision-making for such individuals closely corresponds to decisions made by parents for children. (Indeed, Karen Ann Quinlan's father was designated by the *Quinlan* court to be her medical decision-maker.)

The cases involving infanticide or infant euthanasia follow a similar pattern. This is how the court in the famous Infant Doe of Bloomington, Indiana, case characterized and resolved the matter, holding that Infant Doe's parents could withhold life-saving medical treatment and sustenance from their Down's syndrome child:

> **ISSUE:** Do Mr. and Mrs. Doe, as the natural parents of Infant Doe have the right, after being fully informed of the consequences, to determine the appropriate course of treatment for their minor child?
>
> **CONCLUSION:** It is the opinion of this Court that Mr. and Mrs. Doe, after having been fully informed of the opinions of two sets of physicians, have the right to choose a medically recommended course of treatment for their child in the present circumstances.[32]

The "medically recommended course of treatment" referred to by the court consisted of administration of painkillers and mere palliative care, a regimen known to lead inevitably to the child's death.

---

[31]*Id.* at 13, 355 A.2d at 664.
[32]*In re Guardianship of Infant Doe*, No. GU-824-004A, at 4 (Cir. Ct., Monroe County, Ind., Apr. 12, 1982).

The parental rights cases and cases that involve life issues thus have common themes. Legal controversies on life issues have been largely resolved by expanding the concept of parental rights to encompass life and death decisions over children; legal analogies to the parent-child relation have provided that framework for resolution life and death decisions for adult incompetents.

Moreover, the first illegitimate offspring of the recognized parental right to custody and care of a minor — the right of abortion — has turned on its progenitor and now threatens to overwhelm it and to alter its essential character.

The Minor's Abortion Decision

Consider how the courts have resolved issues that involve potential conflicts between recognized parental rights and the new abortion-privacy right. In 1976, the U.S. Supreme Court initially addressed the question of parental involvement in a minor daughter's abortion. Missouri had enacted a statute that required parental consent for all minors before they could obtain an abortion that was challenged in *Planned Parenthood of Central Missouri v. Danforth*.[33] There, the Court held:

> [The State] does not have the constitutional authority to give a third party an absolute, and possible arbitrary, veto over the decision of the physician and his patient to terminate the patient's pregnancy, regardless of the reason for withholding the consent.[34]

As a consequence, laws that provided parents with full authority to refuse consent for their minor daughter's abortion were deemed unconstitutional. The Court did not, however, foreclose all possibility of parental involvement. It merely held that an

---

[33] 428 U.S. 52 (1976).
[34] *Id.* at 74.

absolute veto power over a minor's decision to abort was unconstitutional, stating that its "holding . . . [did] not suggest that every minor, regardless of age or maturity, may give effective consent for termination of her pregnancy."[35] Thus, the question of whether parental involvement would be permissible in the case of minors incapable of giving effective consent was left open.

Bellotti v. Baird (I),[36] which was before the Supreme Court at the same time as *Danforth*, concerned a Massachusetts statute that provided for parental consent, but also allowed the minor to go into court and obtain judicial consent if her parents refused or if the minor did not wish to approach her parents. The Court declined to rule on this law; instead, it certified the case to the Massachusetts Supreme Court for clarification of the meaning of the statutory provisions.

After some time, the case again made its way to the United States Supreme Court in *Bellotti v. Baird* (II),[37] where the Court then held the law unconstitutional. There was no majority opinion. Four Justices (Powell, Burger, Rehnquist, and Stewart) felt that the statute was unconstitutional because: (1) it permitted a court to overrule a minor's decision to abort even if the court found her to be mature enough to have made the decision in a knowledgeable and informed manner,[38] and (2) it required parental consultation or notification in every instance, without affording the pregnant minor an opportunity to receive an independent judicial determination that she is mature enough to consent or that an abortion would be in her best interests.[39] Four other Justices (Stevens, Marshall, Brennan, and Blackmun)

---

[35]*Id.* at 75.

[36]428 U.S. 132 (1976).

[37]443 U.S. 622 (1979).

[38]*Id.* at 643-44.

[39]*Id.* at 647. Justice Rehnquist, although he concurred in the Powell opinion, joined in it only to provide guidance on the nature of permissible statutes regarding parental involvement, which would have been unavailable if the Court had been more divided. See *id.* at 651 (Rehnquist, J., concurring).

felt that the statute was unconstitutional under *Danforth* because the State had imposed an absolute veto power, either by the minor's parents or by the courts, that applied to every unmarried pregnant minor.[40] Justice White dissented, stating that he would have upheld the statute as written.[41]

Although no majority opinion issued, Justice Powell's plurality opinion concluded:

> . . . that under state regulations such as that undertaken by Massachusetts, every minor must have the opportunity — if she so desires — to go directly to a court without first consulting or notifying her parents. If she satisfies the court that she is mature and well-enough informed to make intelligently the abortion decision on her own, the court must authorize her to act without parental consultation or consent. If she fails to satisfy the court that she is competent to make this decision independently, she must be permitted to show that an abortion nevertheless would be in her best interests. If the court is persuaded that it is, the court must authorize the abortion. If, however, the court is not persuaded by the minor that she is mature or that the abortion would be in her best interests it may decline to sanction the operation.[42]

This position was subsequently vindicated by a full Supreme Court in *Akron, Ashcroft,* and *H.L. v. Matheson.*[43] Here, it settled that a statute that requires parental *consent* prior to abortion is constitutionally permissible if it also provides for a judicial proceeding through which the minor can, without parental consent, procure abortion when it is demonstrated either that the minor is mature enough to make the abortion decision on her own, or, even if she is too immature to make the abortion decision, that the abortion would be in her best interests. Similarly, a law that requires parental *notice* prior to abortion is

---

[40]*Id.* at 652.
[41]*Id.* at 656.
[42]*Id.* at 647-48.
[43]450 U.S. 398 (1981).

constitutionally permissible if it also provides for a judicial proceeding by which the minor can avoid parental knowledge of the abortion if it is demonstrated either that she is mature enough to make the decision on her own or that parental notification would not be in her best interests. Such statutes must also provide that parents cannot be involved in or notified of any judicial proceeding if this would not be in the minor's best interest.

Lower courts, interpreting U.S. Supreme Court precedents, have imposed additional requirements: that the minor's proceedings and any appeal will be expeditious and confidential and that the minor will be provided free counsel.[44]

The concept underlying these decisions, regarding the right of parents to the care, custody, and control of their minor child, is suffused with a deep suspicion of parental influence. That vague and elusive standard — the "best interests" of the minor — has been lifted from the Juvenile Court Acts and given constitutional stature in a manner that the judiciary would never countenance in other contexts. The Juvenile Court Acts themselves permit a "best interest" disposition to be made only *after* some proof of past parental neglect or abuse has been shown.[45] Yet the pattern of decisions in the parental consent and notice to abortion cases assumes a *prospective* determination of abuse or neglect on the part of the parent when informed of the minor's decision; it assumes that the judiciary is somehow better placed than the parents to determine if an abortion is in their daughter's "best interest."

At the heart of the parental right is authority to impress the minor with parental values which the State may not constitutionally evaluate. Surely, if minors have abortion rights, they also have First Amendment rights. Must *Meyer v.*

---

[44]See e.g., *Planned Parenthood v. Bellotti*, 641 F.2d 1006 (1st Cir. 1981); *Wynn v. Carey*, 599 F.2d 193 (7th Cir. 1979).

[45]See e.g., *Ill. Rev. Stat.* ch. 37, sec. 702-4 (1981).

Nebraska,[46] *Pierce v. Society of Sisters,*[47] and *Wisconsin v. Yoder*[48] be recast, then, to require overrulings of parental decisions to instruct children in foreign languages or in particular religious traditions when some judge is convinced that the minor's "best interest" would not be served by such exercises of parental discretion? No doubt, the courts could legitimately overrule even parental decisions of this nature if they jeopardized the child's life. Long-standing case law would support judicial interference in such a circumstance — as, for example, in the familiar case in which Jehovah's Witness parents refuse consent to a blood transfusion for their child. If the very life of the minor were jeopardized by continued pregnancy, then case law might support judicial interference with a parental decision to refuse the minor's abortion. But the parental notice and consent to abortion cases go far beyond this: they wrest discretion away from the parents and place it in the hands of state-actors — members of the judiciary — on the basis of the standardless standard of the minor's "best interests." The court could order that the minor could procure an abortion without parental consent or knowledge on the basis of factors that run contrary to the values that the parents wish to impress upon their child and that have nothing whatever to do with the minor's physical well-being. Indeed, they could order that the parents not be notified of the abortion or even that there has been a hearing on the rectitude of the abortion precisely *because* the parents might react with a renewed effort to impress the minor with their values if they were so notified. They could order that the parents be denied notice of abortion even when the abortion is late in pregnancy and thus represents a more serious threat to the minor's physical integrity than childbirth.

In every instance other than abortion, the courts presume that parents are necessary parties to any determination on the

[46]262 U.S. 390 (1923).
[47]268 U.S. 510 (1925).
[48]406 U.S. 205 (1972).

disposition of a minor. *In re Gault*[49] and *Stanley v. Illinois*,[50] for example, insist that parents be notified of Juvenile Court proceedings that concern their minor child. Yet in *Akron*, the Supreme Court held a law unconstitutional that delegated judicial decisions on a minor's proposed abortion to a Juvenile Court because the Juvenile Court Act of Ohio required that parents must always be notified when a minor comes under Juvenile Court jurisdiction[51] — a requirement no doubt enacted in response to the Supreme Court decisions in *Gault* and *Stanley*. In the case of abortion, however, it is not only not required that parents be notified, it is *unconstitutional* to require that parents be notified of a "best interests" or "mature minor" determination without first determining whether it is in the minor's "best interests" to involve the parents. This determination on whether or not the parents should be notified of the minor's proposed abortion is to occur without any defense of the parental interest — the parents, in essence, may be and, indeed, must be tried and found guilty without any opportunity to defend themselves and without any representation of their interests. Apparently, the Court believes that the Constitution compels this scenario: judges are to determine whether it is the minor's "best interests" to involve the parents merely by listening to the minor and evaluating her uncontroverted rationale why her parents should be kept utterly in the dark about her abortion.

Under the parental notice and consent to abortion cases, the court could find that the minor is mature enough to make her abortion decision on her own, without parental consent or notice, thereby overcoming the usual presumption of the incompetence of the unemancipated minor. One assumes that the minor who is mature enough to make a decision that the Supreme Court itself

---

[49]387 U.S. 1 (1967).
[50]405 U.S. 645 (1972).
[51]*Akron*, 462 U.S. at 469-70.

believes to be "grave"[52] would be mature indeed. Should not such a judicial determination therefore effectively emancipate the minor so that parents no longer have any duties toward them? Yet surely they would be held financially liable for any medical complications that followed the abortion and would be held accountable if they failed to provide her food, clothing, or shelter. If a minor mature enough to make an abortion decision is constitutionally privileged to procure the abortion without parental knowledge or consent, why shouldn't minors mature enough to make *educational* decisions also be able to assert that parents should not be notified of the courses they take or the grades they receive in public schools if such parental knowledge would not be in the minor's "best interest"?

Perhaps the Supreme Court has concocted a special set of rules for the minor's abortion decision — rules that, like the framework of *Roe* itself, represent a legislative rather than judicial solution to perceived conflicting interests and values. Or perhaps the framework established in these cases does not merely represent judicial caprice but has broader applications. If it applies to the minor's abortion right, why not the minor's free speech and religious rights? Or to educational decisions that are aspects of these rights? Their right to be sterilized? Their right to travel?

In either case, these decisions represent a clear curtailment of the traditional parental rights to care and control of minor children in the context of reproductive and sexual decision-making. If their principles were applied in other contexts, they would foment a true legal revolution in the nature of family relations with regard to older children. Parental decision-making on the most fundamental childrearing issues could be overridden or short-circuited merely if it were determined that the minor was supposedly mature enough to make a contrary decision, or, in any

---

[52]*Bellotti v. Baird* (II), 443 U.S. 662, 641 (1979), quoting *Planned Parenthood of Central Missouri v. Danforth*, 428 U.S. 52, 91 (1976), (Stewart, J., concurring).

event, if some judge believed the parents' view did not serve the minor's best interest.

The Father's Interest

The recognition of a right to abortion threatens to subsume parental rights with respect to minor children. It also threatens to create an absurd imbalance as between the rights and interests of the parents — a skewed and distorted concept of the relative weight to be accorded to the father and to the mother in relation to their unborn child.

Roe v. Wade held that there exists a zone of privacy encapsuling the woman and her physician that protects their abortion decision. But surely there is a missing element: the father plainly has a manifest interest in the disposition of his unborn child. His recognized procreative, reproductive, and parental rights and interests are at stake. May the State require that the father be given the power to consent to the abortion? Or at least to know that it occurs?

So far, the answer to the first question is almost always "no" and to the second a tentative and qualified "yes."

The leading cases concerning the relative weight to be accorded the views of the father and mother of an unborn child have also involved the spousal relation — they have concerned the relative weight accorded to the views of the *husband* and *wife*. The unwed father received some legal attention, but his case is considerably weaker than that of the husband. Introduction of the element of a marital relation permits the State to assert on behalf of the male not only interests in protecting the male's procreative and parental rights in the context of abortion, but also an interest in regulating the integrity of the marital relation. Moreover, in absence of a marital relationship, which raises the presumption that every child conceived of the marriage is the husband's, the male might have difficulty in asserting procreative and parental rights. Would he be able to prove that a particular unborn child was his own?

The husband's interest in a proposed abortion was first considered in *Planned Parenthood v. Danforth* in the context of considering the constitutionality of a Missouri statute that provided for the consent of the husband before any abortion could be performed on a married woman. The U.S. Supreme Court invalidated the law, stating that:

> [It] does much more than insure that the husband participate in the decision whether his wife should have an abortion. . . . The State, [rather,] has granted him the right to prevent unilaterally, and for whatever reason, the effectuation of his wife's and her physician's decision to terminate her pregnancy. This state determination not only may discourage the consultation that might normally be expected to precede a major decision affecting the marital couple but also, and more importantly, the State has interposed an absolute obstacle to a woman's decision that *Roe* held to be constitutionally protected from such interference.[53]

The Court implied that the State can logically only provide the husband with "veto power" over abortion when the State itself has that power. Does this mean that the State can only provide the husband with the power to consent after fetal viability has been attained and when abortion can be proscribed by the State (except for reasons of maternal life or health)?[54] There is little impetus to enact a statute of such limited import in view of the relatively few number of abortions performed at this late stage of pregnancy and, more importantly, because abortions after viability can be banned in any event. This seemingly implacable blank wall constructed by the court has discouraged any explicit spousal consent legislation since *Danforth*.

---

[53]*Danforth*, 428 U.S. at 70-71 n. 11.
[54]*Roe v. Wade*, 410 U.S. at 164-65.

A few States have, however, enacted laws that at least require notice to the spouse prior to abortion: Florida,[55] Rhode Island,[56] and Utah.[57] The most important precedent in this regard was provided through litigation of the Florida law in *Scheinberg v. Smith*.[58] There a federal Court of Appeals in essence upheld the concept of spousal notice, stating that:

> [B]y creating marriage as the vehicle for legally safeguarded family life, the state has made the marital partners entirely dependent on each other for fulfillment of familial aspirations. If either partner is to enjoy one of the primary purposes of marriage, the bringing forth and nurturing of children, each partner must cooperate in matters of childbirth. (Citation omitted.) Most assuredly the state does not have the right to require, as an incident of marriage, the fulfillment of each spouse's procreative desires. (Citation omitted.) The state does, however, have a substantial interest in attempting to ensure that the state-created vehicle for procreation, marriage, not be abused through one spouse perpetually and secretively frustrating the other's desire for offspring. All Florida has decided is that, if a woman wishes to forego childbirth, she must notify her partner in family life. Her husband has legally committed himself to a contractual relationship that prohibits the extra-marital creation of children. If his aspirations include a desire for children, it is a small concession for him to have the right to know that his wife is considering an abortion. The marital relationship is the only legitimate vehicle the husband presently has for realizing his procreative rights. The husband's ability to procreate, moreover, is entitled to constitutional protection. (Citation omitted.) The state, therefore, has a compelling interest in requiring a wife to inform her husband when she is contemplating termination of a pregnancy. Absent such a right the marital relationship between a couple could be maintained without a husband ever discovering why or how

---

[55]*Fla. Stat. Ann.*, sec. 390.001(4)(b) (West 1986).
[56]*R.I. Gen. Laws*, sec. 23-4.8-1 to 23-4.8-5 (1985).
[57]*Utah Code Ann.*, sec. 76-7-304 (Supp. 1987).
[58]659 F.2d 476 (5th Cir. 1981).

> his aspirations for a family have been frustrated. This is
> surely a perversion of the institution of marriage, as
> conceived in our society and as instituted by the state.[59]

Though the State's interests were deemed sufficiently
"compelling" to warrant a spousal notice law, the court remained
uncertain whether such a statute was "narrowly drawn" in that it
required notice even when the husband was not the father of the
child.[60] Thus, the court remanded the case to the district court to
determine whether abortion caused any significant impact on the
reproductive capacity of a marriage (as through sterility,
subsequent miscarriage, or subsequent premature birth).[61] If so,
then the notice requirement would have been warranted even if
the husband were not the father of the child. The lower court
found no such impact and, hence, held the law unconstitutional.[62]
Nevertheless, a carefully crafted law that provided an exception
for the case when the husband is not the father, or that provided
for a judicial procedure in which the wife could prove that he is
not the father and thence forego notification, would evidently
pass muster under this federal appellate court decision.

The narrow analytic framework that the Supreme Court
employed in foreclosing spousal consent laws assumed that the
State is the sole source of rights and interests sufficient to
override abortion decisions. Because the State had no such
authority, it had no power to impute to the husband or father.
This exceedingly myopic form of reasoning overlooked the
possibility that the husband's or father's procreative and parental
interests arise from a source independent from state authority
and the possibility that the addition of the *new* element of the
husband or father to the abortion formula might create a *new*
power in the State or its courts that would warrant protection of

---

[59]*Id.* at 485.
[60]*Id.* at 486.
[61]*Id.* at 487.
[62]*Scheinberg v. Smith*, 550 F. Supp. 1112 (S.D. Fla. 1982).

the husband's or father's rights and interests. If the rights the husband or father has at stake in a decision to abort his child are fundamental in character, does not the State maintain a compelling interest in protecting them by law?

After all, before a child is to be placed for adoption even an unwed father must, under the Constitution, be provided with an opportunity to assume custody.[63] Why, then, is it *always* constitutionally forbidden to require spousal or parental consent before the life of his unborn child is taken? Although, as *Danforth* proclaims, the exercise of "absolute" paternal veto power over abortion is not permissible, might not the balance be tipped in the father's favor, at least when the woman's reason for abortion is demonstrably trivial? Such an approach, which would urge the courts to balance, on a case by case basis, the rights and interests of father/husband and mother/wife, represents the most recent efforts to provide the male with some modicum of justice and procreative equality.[64]

Thus far, however, parental rights — this time, those of the father — have been illogically subsumed by the new-found "parental right" of the mother to procure an abortion. In Roman law, the father of a family could compel the abortion of his wife under the aegis of *paterfamilias*, notwithstanding maternal objections. The reverse is now true in American law, which provides that a doctrine of intrauterine *materfamilias* be recognized under the Constitution — a perversely absurd result in view of the values undoubtedly held by its Framers.

---

[63]*Stanley v. Illinois*, 405 U.S. 645 (1972).

[64]*John Doe v. Jane Smith*, No. 20-D0288-OS-JP-095 (Cir. Ct., Elkhart County, Ind., 1988), *on appeal*, No. 20800-8806-CU-551 (Ind. 1988); *Conn v. Conn*, No. 73C01-8806-DR-127 (Cir. Ct., Shelby County, Ind., 1988), *on appeal*, No. 73A-1-8806-CU-0021 (Ind. Ct. App., Div. 1, 1988); *Jane Doe v. John Smith*, No. 84C01-8804-JP-185 (Cir. Ct., Vigo County, Ind., 1988), *on appeal*, No. 84A01-8804-CU-00112 (Ind. Ct. App., Div. 1, 1988).

The crux of the Court's holding that wives, and not husbands, are constitutionally authorized to make unilateral abortion decisions is that wives are the "bearers of the burden" of continued pregnancy.[65] The logic of this rationale, if extended to legal issues encompassing burgeoning reproductive technology, mocks the mutual parental and procreative interests of both the male and female. The "bearer of the burden" of a child conceived *in vitro*, or who is nurtured by an artificial womb, or who is borne by a surrogate parent, is the one who pays the bills. Is whether such a child lives or dies to be a matter to be decided solely by the parent who has sufficient financial resources to afford the technology involved? Such a scenario reduces the very young human being to a mere chattel of the financially secure parent. Yet, such a repugnant legal conclusion is logically consistent with the rationale the Court employed determining that the husband cannot prevent a wife's abortion because the "cost" to the wife of continued pregnancy was deemed always to outweigh any "benefit" the child might represent to the husband.

Infanticide

The relationship to which the right to abortion attaches is that of the woman to her physician; the relationship to which the newly developing right to deny treatment to a disabled child attaches is that of the parents of the child to the child's physician.

Usual principles of law would obviously foreclose parental decisions to deny life-saving treatment, nutrition, and hydration to their child. Homicide and child neglect statutes provide no exceptions for instances in which parents are the offenders or in which a child born with a mental or physical disability is the victim. If it is desirable to permit or to immunize conduct that would cause the death of the child, therefore, some new legal

---

[65]*Danforth*, 428 U.S. at 71.

principle must be introduced that would prevent application of the usual rules. The development of a constitutional doctrine that overrides statutory and common law is a ready solution. In essence, such a doctrine would consist of a parental right to decide which alternative forms of "treatment" should be accorded a disabled child, even if the treatment selected would result in the child's death.

Although such a "right" has yet to be plainly and expansively articulated by the courts, it obviously lurks in the decision of the Bloomington, Indiana, court that permitted the parents of Infant Doe to choose pain-killers and palliative care in preference to curative, available, and relatively safe surgery to repair their Down's syndrome child's tracheoesophageal fistula. It is implied in the decisions of the courts striking the "Infant Doe" regulations issued to protect such children from similar decisions.[66] The birth of a disabled child — particularly a child who is presumed to be retarded — is conceived to create a special circumstance that warrants the creation of a constitutional doctrine that would immunize a parental decision resulting in the child's avoidable death.

The transparently self-serving nature of such reasoning is apparent. There is no doubt that the courts would compel life-saving treatment for a child whose parents do not favor him because of race or sex. Parental religious scruples would not be permitted to override a child's need for treatment. In such cases, a parental assertion that they are merely choosing an "alternative form of treatment" (that incidentally will lead inexorably to death) over a form of treatment that would save the child's life would be viewed precisely for what it is: an utterly disingenuous pretext. The expressed or implied assertion of any such parental "right" is obviously intended to mask an underlying judgment

---

[66]See generally *Bowen v. American Hospital Association*, 476 U.S. 610 (1986); *American Medical Association v. Heckler*, 585 F. Supp. 541 (S.D.N.Y. 1984); *American Academy of Pediatrics v. Heckler*, 561 F. Supp. 395 (D.D.C. 1983).

that, in the circumstance of a disabled newborn, the parental decision to bring about the child's death is correct — and correct precisely because the child is deemed unworthy, on account of his disability, of the protection the law would otherwise accord him. To invoke the parental right to nurture and to care for the child as a justification to deprive them of food, water, and available life-saving treatment perverts the law and mocks the very purpose for which parents were acknowledged to be possessors of such a right in the first place.

Consider how this matter would be dealt with if the judiciary were as concerned with the right to life of the disabled infant explicitly acknowledged in the Constitution as it is with the alleged right of the minor to procure abortion without parental knowledge or consent.

The pregnant minor, no matter how immature, can procure an abortion without parental consent if it is deemed by a court to be in the minor's "best interests." Simple embarrassment over an out-of-wedlock pregnancy might be sufficient to meet this test. But the parents of a disabled infant in need of life-saving treatment or sustenance have a right to choose a "treatment option" that inevitably means the infant's death. If the same treatment standard were applied to the disabled infant as to the pregnant minor, then the judiciary would order treatment and sustenance for the infant, because this is plainly in the infant's "best interest," and put aside any parental preference that would result in death.

The pregnant minor, no matter how immature, can procure an abortion without notice to her parents if parental knowledge is deemed opposed to the minor's "best interest." But when it is claimed that a disabled newborn is being denied life-saving treatment, the government cannot even secure access to the child's medical records over parental objections in order to determine whether the treatment or lack of treatment the child is receiving violates the law.[67] Information forbidden to the parents in the first case is regarded as their exclusive possession in the second.

Obviously, such inconsistent results cannot be explained by reference to any special concern for parental rights. Rather, they represent an implicit judgment that disabled children are members of a legally disfavored class. Thus, parental rights and prerogatives are once more employed as a mere pretext to achieve an approved and unrelated end — here, the demise of disabled children. And once more is the integrity of the concept of parental rights and prerogatives perverted: a parental "right to infanticide" is a right debased.

Conclusion

A proper view of the nature of parental rights would acknowledge appropriate limitations on their exercise and insist on an even-handed application of the legal principles they embody to all circumstances. As has been shown, parental rights cannot properly be extended to protect decisions that result in the death of children, born or unborn. The development of legal precedents that represent a parental right that, in essence, warrants such parental decision-making creates glaring and irrational inconsistencies in the way the law treats parental prerogatives in different circumstances. Moreover, these precedents threaten to vitiate long recognized parental prerogatives and interests if extended in a consistent fashion to encompass other situations.

There is no necessary conflict between parental rights and the right of young human beings to continued existence. The conflict that presently exists can be traced directly to judicial

---

[67]*Bowen*, 476 U.S. at 622 [*United States v. University Hospital, State Univ. of N.Y. at Stony Brook*, 575 F. Supp. 607, 614 (E.D.N.Y. 1983), *aff'd* 729 F.2d 144 (1984)].

debasement of the concept of parental rights, extending them beyond their proper scope in order to employ them as a pretext to permit the death of children in the womb and children born with physical or mental disabilities. This result-orientated jurisprudence must cease if the law is to provide protection both for the weakest among us and for legitimate parental aspirations.

Parental Rights and Education

Charles E. Rice

The topic of this paper deserves a multi-volume treatise. The limited purpose here, however, is not to examine parental rights in detail, but merely to note some respects in which they are challenged today and, especially, to urge a renewed emphasis on the rights and duties of parents as the primary educators.

Parents indeed have rights in education prior to those of the state. As the Supreme Court said in 1925 in striking down a state requirement that all children attend public schools, "[t]he child is not the mere creature of the State."[1] This reality was emphasized by the Second Vatican Council which declared that, "Parents have the primary and inalienable duty of educating their children, and must enjoy true freedom in choosing schools."[2] Unfortunately, the primacy of the parental right over the education of children is endangered by several tendencies today. One, of course, is the disintegration of the family itself, as evidenced by the high divorce rate with its dislocation of children and weakening of natural parental bonds. Another is economic pressure, on account of which too many parents find it impossible to exercise the right to educate which for them has, therefore, become merely theoretical. Of necessity, they send their children to public schools over which they have little or no control.

---

[1] *Pierce v. Society of Sisters*, 268 U.S. 510, 535 (1925).
[2] Second Vatican Council, Declaration on Christian Education, No. 5.

In the colonial period and the early decades of the Republic, elementary and secondary education was religious and was primarily a function of the Church:

> Traditionally, organized education in the Western world was Church education. It could hardly be otherwise when the education of children was primarily study of the Word and the way of God. Even in the Protestant countries, where there was a less close identification of Church and State, the basis of education was largely the Bible, and its chief purpose inculcation of piety. To the extent that the State intervened, it used its authority to further aims of the Church.
>
> The emigrants who came to these shores brought this view of education with them. Colonial schools certainly started with a religious orientation. When the common problems of the early settlers of the Massachusetts Bay Colony revealed the need for common schools, the object was the defeat of "one chief project of that old deluder, Satan, to keep men from the knowledge of the Scriptures."[3]

The early public schools were, as one scholar states, "sectarian public schools, where the public supported a single established religion and where dissenters' schools were not allowed to function."[4] The first public school law in the colonies, the "old deluder" statute enacted by Massachusetts in 1647, required every town of more than fifty householders to provide a schoolmaster to teach the children to read the Scriptures.[5]

Through the early decades after independence, even public schools continued to be quite sectarian.[6] The public school

---

[3]*McCollum v. Board of Education*, 333 U.S. 203, 213-214 (1948) [Frankfurter, J., concurring and quoting *The Laws and Liberties of Massachusetts*, 47 (1648)].

[4]Boles, D., *The Bible, Religion, and the Public Schools*, 4 (1965).

[5]See Stokes, A., *Church and State in the United States*, 50 (1950).

[6]See Connors, E., *Church-State Relationships in Education in the State of New York* (1983), note 12, at xv; 6 New York State

movement began to grow in the 1830's and 1840's, particularly through the influence of Horace Mann's movement for "nonsectarian" public schools in which the "common truths" of Christianity would be taught, including the Bible and an overlay of common denominator Protestantism.[7] Protestant support for these schools increased as Catholic opposition to their Protestant characteristics grew.[8] After the Civil War, the conflict was resolved through a general arrangement, whereby public funds would not be used for any denominational schools, but the public schools would retain their prayer, Bible reading, and other trappings of common denominator Protestantism.[9] The Blaine Amendment, proposed in 1875 by President Grant, embodied this solution. The Blaine Amendment never received the necessary two-thirds majorities in Congress and, therefore, was never referred to the states for ratification. Nevertheless, similar provisions were incorporated in the constitutions of 29 states between 1877 and 1917.[10]

This compromise endured through the first quarter or so of the twentieth century. But in the 1930's, 1940's, and 1950's, secularist opposition to the indicia of religion in public schools became stronger, culminating in the Supreme Court's school

---

Constitutional Convention Committee Report 229-30 (1938); Stokes, A., *supra*, note 14, at 52-54.

[7]See Stokes, A., *supra*, 53-54.

[8]See *Commonwealth v. Cooke*, 7 *Am. L. Req.*, 417, 423 (Boston, Mass., Police Ct. 1959); see also *Donahoe v. Richards*, 38 Me. 376 (1854) (upholding the expulsion of a Catholic child from a public school for refusal to read in class the Protestant version of the Bible).

[9]Stokes, A., *supra*, note 14, at 69-71; Jorgenson, "The Birth of a Tradition," *Phi Delta Kappa* (June 1983), note 23, at 413.

[10]See Boles, D., *supra*, note 10, at 30-32; 4 *Cong. Rec.* 175, 205, 5453 (1875-1876); Proposed Amendments to the Constitution, H.R. Doc. No. 551, 70th Cong., 2nd Sess. 182 (1928); Stokes, A., Pfeffer, L., *Church and State in the United States*, 272 (1964); Zollmar, C., *American Church Law*, 75-76 (1933); Meyer, A., *The Blaine Amendment and the Bill of Rights*, 64 *Harv. L. Rev.* 939 (1951).

prayer decisions of 1962 and 1963.[11] Under those decisions and their elaborations by the Supreme Court, the state and federal governments are required to maintain neutrality between theism and non-theism, an impossible task. In *Torcaso v. Watkins*, the Supreme Court declared: "We repeat and again reaffirm that neither a State nor the Federal Government can constitutionally force a person 'to profess a belief or disbelief in any religion.' Neither can constitutionally pass laws or impose requirements which aid all religions as against non-believers, and neither can aid all religions as against non-believers, and neither can aid those religions based on a belief in the existence of God as against those religions founded on different beliefs."[12] In a footnote to the last quoted clause, the Court stated, "Among religions in this country which do not teach what would commonly be considered a belief in the existence of God are Buddhism, Taoism, Ethical Culture, Secular Humanism and others."[13]

Under this criterion, any affirmation by government of the truth of theism would be unconstitutional. Only if such an affirmation is merely symbolic will it be allowed. Thus, in the 1963 school prayer case, Justice Brennan, in concurrence, noted that the words 'under God' in the revised Pledge of Allegiance are not necessarily unconstitutional because they "may merely recognize the historical fact that our Nation was believed to have been founded 'under God.'"[14] As a result of this neutrality mandate, public schools must avoid not only prayer but also all affirmations of religious and moral truth. This false neutrality is the origin of the justified parental complaints on the public school treatment of the moral issues involved in sex education and similar programs. Objecting parents have tried without

---

[11]See *Abington School Dist. v. Schempp*, 374 U.S. 203 (1963); *Engle v. Vitale*, 370 U.S. 421 (1962).

[12]*Torcaso v. Watkins*, 367 U.S. 488, 495 (1961).

[13]*Ibid.*, at 495, note 11.

[14]374 U.S. at 304.

success to have the objectionable courses removed from the curriculum and to have their children excused from such programs to which they have religious objections.[15] Excusal of objecting students, according to the courts, is a matter for the discretion of the school board; it is not available as a matter of constitutional right.

Two recent U.S. District Court cases illustrate the theoretical and practical issues raised by parental objections to alleged secular humanism in public schools. In *Mozert v. Hawkins County Public Schools*,[16] fundamentalist Christian parents objected to the compulsory use of the 1983 edition of the Holt, Rinehart and Winston basic reading series in the public schools. "It is important to note at the outset," said the court, "that the plaintiffs are not requesting that the Holt series be banned from the classroom nor are they seeking to expunge the theory of evolution from the public school curriculum."[17] The parents sought to recover the expenses incurred by sending their children to private schools, and they sought an order requiring the public schools to provide alternative reading instruction.

The parents objected to the Holt series because, for example, it "contains a definite feminist theme, and the plaintiffs have a religious objection to stories which appear to denigrate the differences between the sexes. . . . The plaintiffs believe that, after reading the entire Holt series, a child might adopt the views of a feminist, a humanist, a pacifist, and an anti-Christian, a vegetarian, or an advocate of a 'one-world government.' Plaintiffs sincerely believe that the repetitive affirmation of these philosophical viewpoints is repulsive to the Christian faith — so repulsive that they must not allow their children to be exposed to the Holt series."[18]

---

[15]See *Davis v. Page*, 385 F. Supp. 395 (D.N.H., 1974).
[16]647 F. Supp. 1194 (E.D. Tenn. 1986).
[17]647 F. Supp. at 1195.
[18]647 F. Supp. at 1199.

District Judge Thomas Hull found that the state unconstitutionally burdened the free exercise of the plaintiffs' religion by requiring "that the student-plaintiffs either read the offensive texts or give up their free public education."[19] The court rejected the school board's contention that to give relief to these plaintiffs would open "the flood gates" to similar requests.[20] Rather, the court emphasized that the plaintiffs "have not made multi-subject, multi-text objections; they have objected to the Holt reading series. The defendants may not justify burdening the plaintiffs' free exercise rights in this narrow case on the basis of what the plaintiffs might find objectionable in the future."[21] The court ordered the school board to permit "the student-plaintiffs to opt out of reading class. . . . [E]ach of the student-plaintiffs would withdraw to a study hall or to the library during his or her regular reading period at school and would study reading with a parent later at home."[22]

If parents find the public schools objectionable for religious reasons, they have a right to educate their children in private schools or, depending on state law, at home. The problem presented by the suit in *Mozert*, however, is whether the state's compelling interest in educating effectively the children who do attend the public schools will justify a burden on the free exercise rights of students who object to part of the curriculum by requiring them either to participate in the full curriculum or to leave school entirely. The plaintiffs in *Mozert* did not seek to have the Holt series removed from the schools. It was instead a narrow, free exercise of religion case. The broader issue, however, was presented in *Smith v. Board of School Commissioners of Mobile County*, in which U.S. District Judge W. Brevard Hand, in Alabama, ordered various social studies, history and economics texts removed from the public schools on

---

[19]647 F. Supp. at 1200.
[20]647 F. Supp. at 1202.
[21]647 F. Supp. at 1201.
[22]647 F. Supp. at 1203.

the ground that they unconstitutionally promote a religion of secular humanism. "These history books," said Judge Hand, "discriminate against the very concept of religion, and theistic religions in particular, by omissions so serious that a student learning history from them would not be apprised of relevant facts about America's history."[23]

Judge Hand stated that for "purposes of the First Amendment, secular humanism is a religious belief system, entitled to the protections of, and subject to the prohibitions of, the religion clauses. It is not a mere scientific methodology that may be promoted and advanced in the public schools."[24] "As already noted, the Supreme Court has declared that teaching religious tenets in such a way as to promote or encourage a religion violates the religion clauses [of the Constitution]. This prohibition is not implicated by mere coincidence of ideas with religious tenets," Judge Hand said. "Rather, there must be a systematic, whether explicit or implicit, promotion of a belief system as a whole. The facts showed that the state of Alabama has on its state textbook list certain volumes that are being used by school systems in this state, which engage in such promotion."[25]

The decision was epitomized by Judge Hand's conclusion that, "If this court is compelled to purge 'God is great, God is good, we thank Him for our daily food' from the classroom, then this court must also purge from the classroom those things that serve to teach that salvation is through one's self rather than through a deity."[26] Significantly, Judge Hand ruled that textbooks could not be held to involve an unconstitutional establishment of religion because of "mere coincidence" between positions taken in the book and the positions affirmed by a particular religion.

---

[23]N.Y. Times, March 5, 1987, p. 1, col. 1.
[24]N.Y. Times, March 5, 1987, p. 1, col. 1.
[25]Washington Times, March 5, 1987, p. 3A, col. 5.
[26]N.Y. Times, March 5, 1987, p. 1, col. 1.

Although there could be difficulty in drawing a line, he held that the state had overstepped its bounds in that case:

> The question arises how public schools can deal with topics that overlap with areas covered by religious belief. Mere coincidence between a statement in a textbook and a religious belief is not an establishment of religion. However, some religious beliefs are so fundamental that the act of denying them will completely undermine that religion. In addition, denial of that belief will result in the affirmance of a contrary belief and result in the establishment of an opposing religion.
>
> Teaching that moral choices are purely personal and can only be based on some autonomous, as yet undiscovered and unfulfilled, inner self is a sweeping fundamental belief that must not be promoted by the public schools. The state can, of course, teach the law of the land, which is that each person is responsible for and will be held to account for, his actions. There is a distinct practical consequence between this fact, and the religious belief promoted, whether explicitly or implicitly, by saying "only you can decide what is right and wrong." With these books the State of Alabama has overstepped its mark, and must withdraw to perform its proper nonreligious functions.[27]

Judge Hand's ruling, of course, raised by implication the issue of whether public education itself is unconstitutional as a violation of the neutrality toward religion required by the Establishment Clause of the First Amendment. "The essence of education," wrote Alfred North Whitehead, "is that it be religious."[28] Education, like jurisprudence, is, in a sense, an exercise in "ultimatology."[29] Since the 1920's, the religion of the public schools has changed from a common denominator Protestantism to a secular humanism which excludes any

---

[27]N.Y. Times, March 7, 1987, p. 7, col. 5.

[28]Whitehead, A., *The Aims of Education* (1929), 25.

[29]See Barrett, E., "Lawyer Looks at Natural Law Jurisprudence," 23 *Am. J. Juris* 1 (1978).

affirmation of God and His law and which implicitly promotes a relativistic morality that is hostile to Christian beliefs. Whatever the theoretical constitutionality of public education, the aggressively secular character of those schools has prompted an increasing number of parents to forsake the public schools entirely. There is a "broad national movement in which growing numbers of parents have chosen one of two paths of resistance to state control. One group simply chooses to teach its children at home. There are now about a million such home-taught children, many of whose parents have acted for religious reasons," according to Christopher Klicka, executive director of the Home School Legal Defense Association, a support group of lawyers with about 5000 dues-paying families as members. "There are still more students, perhaps as many as six million, who belong to church schools, many of which have state approval and state certification of their teachers. But many others in that group attend schools, often run by fundamentalist Christian churches... that shun state certification on religious and philosophical grounds."[30]

It has been reliably estimated that "between eight and ten thousand Christian day schools have been established since the mid 1960's, with a current enrollment of approximately one million students."[31] Another study described these schools as follows:

> The growth in Christian schools is truly one of the most significant cultural phenomena of the decade. By and large the students come from lower-middle-class families whose incomes lie in the ten thousand to fifteen thousand dollar range. Despite the often heard criticism that Christian school growth has been motivated by racial prejudice, the reality is just the opposite. Less than 5 percent of these private schools are segregationist oriented. The over-

---

[30]N.Y. Times, March 25, 1987, p. 1, col. 2.
[31]Carper, "The Christian Day School Movement, 1960-1982," 17 *Educ. F.* 135 (1983).

whelming majority are deeply committed to fostering integration between the races.

There is no doubt that the mushrooming growth in evangelical believers, evangelical communications, and evangelical infrastructures is the most significant cultural phenomenon in American life today.[32]

As the Supreme Court stated, in Christian schools "[t]he church-teacher relationship . . . differs from the employment relationship in a public or other nonreligious school."[33] The Supreme Court has "recognized the critical and unique role of the teacher in fulfilling the mission of a church-operated school."[34] His or her task is not a job; it is a religious vocation:

> Our schools are not only religious in the sense that religion is the motive for their existence. Each is in fact a pervasively religious ministry ministering in Christ's name. Curriculum is profoundly influenced by Biblical insights. Teaching methods are Bibliocentric. Codes of discipline and standards of dress are derived from Biblical require-ments. The schools are, in a true sense, communities of faith — in which conduct and manners, learning and teaching, recreation and all personal relationships, are completely infused with the implications of Christian teaching. The teachers in our schools pursue their religious vocations at personal sacrifice and solely for their love of Jesus Christ.[35]

---

[32]Rifkin, Jeremy, *The Emerging Order: God in the Age of Scarcity* (1979), 122, 126.

[33]*NLRB v. Catholic Bishop of Chicago*, 440 U.S. 490, 504 (1979).

[34]*Ibid.* at 501; see also, *Lemon v. Kurtzman*, 403 U.S. 602, 616, 635 (1971) and *Meek v. Pittenger*, 421 U.S. 349, 365 (1985), on the pervasively religious character of teaching in church-related schools.

[35]Testimony of Paul A. Kienel, Executive Director, Association of Christian Schools International, at Hearing Before United States Senate Committee on Finance on Mandatory Social Security Coverage for Employees of Religious Organizations, Washington, D.C., December 14, 1983.

The constitutional status of Christian schools depends upon a delicate balancing of the interests of the schools, the students, their parents, the teachers, and the administrators against the important interest of the state in the development of an educated citizenry. The importance of the parental right with respect to education was established by the Supreme Court six decades ago.[36] In *Meyer v. Nebraska*, the Supreme Court held that, "[a teacher's] right to teach and the right of parents to engage him so to instruct their children . . . are within the liberty of the [Fourteenth] Amendment."[37] And in *Pierce v. Society of Sisters*, the Court stated:

> The fundamental theory of liberty upon which all governments in this Union repose excludes any general power of the State to standardize its children by forcing them to accept instruction from public teachers only. The child is not the mere creature of the State; those who nurture him and direct his destiny have the right, coupled with the high duty, to recognize and prepare him for additional obligations. [See also *Farrington v. Tokushige*, where the Court held unconstitutional a law which sought to promote "Americanism" among pupils attending foreign language schools in Hawaii. The Court held that the regulations violated the parents' due process rights and their right to control their children's education.][38]

The parental right to control the education of children is, of course, not unlimited.[39] Nevertheless, the Supreme Court has stated that "[t]he parental interest in the direction and control of a child's education is central to the family's constitutionally

---

[36]See, generally, "Note, Parental Rights: Educational Alternatives and Curriculum Control," 36 *Wash. and Lee L. Rev.*, 277 (1979).

[37]262 U.S. 390, 400 (1923).

[38]268 U.S. 510, 535 (1925). See also *Farrington v. Tokushige*, 273 U.S. 284, 293, 298 (1927).

[39]See *Pierce v. Society of Sisters*, 268 U.S. at 534; *Farrington v. Tokushige*, 273 U.S. at 298-99; *Board of Education v. Allen*, 392 U.S. 236, 245-46 (1968); *Runyon v. McCrary*, 427 U.S. 160, 179-80 (1976).

protected family rights" and "[t]he state's power to control the education of its citizens is secondary to the rights of parents 'to provide an equivalent education for their children in a privately operated school of [their] choice.' *Norwood v. Harrison*, 413 U.S. 455, 461. . . ."[40] The Court has also acknowledged that the primacy of the parental right, even though it is not absolute, is a reflection of the reality "that the custody, care and nurture of the child reside first in the parents, whose primary function and freedom include preparation for obligations the state can neither supply nor hinder."[41]

In *Cleveland Board of Education v. LaFleur*, the Court emphasized that the parental right over education is an aspect of the "freedom of personal choice in matters of marriage and family life" which is protected by the Due Process Clause of the Fourteenth Amendment.[42] As Justice Powell observed in his plurality opinion in *Moore v. East Cleveland*, "A host of cases, tracing their lineage to *Meyer v. Nebraska*, . . . and *Pierce v. Society of Sisters*, . . . have consistently acknowledged a 'private realm of family life which the state cannot enter.' *Prince v. Mass.*, . . . *Roe v. Wade*, 410 U.S. 113 (1973) . . . *Wisconsin v. Yoder*, . . . *Stanley v. Illinois*, 405 U.S. 645 (1972) . . . *Ginsberg v. New York*, 390 U.S. 629 (1968) . . . *Griswold v. Connecticut*, 381 U.S. 479 (1965) . . . *Poe v. Ullman*, 367 U.S. 497 (1961) . . . cf. *Loving v. Virginia*, 388 U.S. 1 (1967) . . . *May v. Anderson*, 345 U.S. 528 (1953) . . . *Skinner v. Oklahoma ex rel. Williamson*, 316 U.S. 535 (1942) . . . Of course, the family is not beyond regulation. See *Prince v. Massachusetts*. . . . But when the government intrudes on choices concerning family living arrangements, *this Court must examine*

---

[40]*Brantley v. Surles*, 718 F.2d 1354, 1358-59 (5th Cir. 1983).

[41]*Prince v. Massachusetts*, 321 U.S. 158, 166 (1944); see also *Lehr v. Robertson*, 103 S. Ct. 2985, 2991 (1983).

[42]*Cleveland Board of Educ. v. LaFleur*, 414 U.S. 632, 639-40 (1974).

carefully the importance of the governmental interests advanced and the extent to which they are served by the challenged regulation."[43]

This important parental right over education is at its strongest when it is joined with the preferred right to the free exercise of religion:

> Thus, a State's interest in universal education, however highly we rank it, is not totally free from a balancing process when it impinges on fundamental rights and interests, such as those specifically protected by the Free Exercise Clause of the First Amendment, and the traditional interest of parents with respect to the religious upbringing of their children so long as they, in the words of *Pierce*, "prepare [them] for additional obligations."[44]

> It follows that in order for Wisconsin to compel school attendance beyond the eighth grade against a claim that such attendance interferes with the practice of a legitimate religious belief, it must appear either that the State does not deny the free exercise of religious belief by its requirement, or that there is a state interest of sufficient magnitude to override the interest claiming protection under the Free Exercise Clause. . . . The essence of all that has been said and written on the subject is that *only those interests of the highest order and those not otherwise served can overbalance legitimate claims to the free exercise of religion.*[45]

Religious freedom may be limited by government only upon proof of a "compelling state interest."[46] The Supreme Court has said that while "[t]he state may justify an inroad on religious liberty by showing that it is the least restrictive means of achieving some compelling state interest,"[47] "only those interests

---

[43]*Moore v. East Cleveland*, 431 U.S. 494, 499 (1977) (emphasis added).

[44]268 U.S., at 535 L. Ed. at 1078.

[45]*Wisconsin v. Yoder*, 406 U.S. 205, 214-215 (1972) (emphasis added).

[46]*Sherbert v. Verner*, 374 U.S. 398, 406 (1963).

[47]*Thomas v. Review Board*, 450 U.S. 706, 718 (1981).

of the highest order and those not otherwise served can overbalance legitimate claims to the free exercise of religion."[48]

Wisconsin v. Yoder involved what the Court described as "the fundamental interest of parents, as contrasted with that of the State, to guide the religious future and education of their children. The history and culture of Western civilization reflect a strong tradition of parental concern for the nurture and upbringing of their children. This primary role of the parents in the upbringing of their children is now established beyond debate as an enduring American tradition."[49] The Court in *Yoder* stressed the special protection afforded to the parental right to educate when its exercise is religiously motivated:

> *Pierce*, of course, recognized that where nothing more than the general interest of the parent in the nurture and education of his children is involved, it is beyond dispute that the State acts "reasonably" and constitutionally in requiring education to age 16 in some public or private school meeting the standards prescribed by the State.
>
> However read, the Court's holding in *Pierce* stands as a charter of the rights of parents to direct the religious upbringing of their children. And, *when the interests of parenthood are combined with a free exercise claim of the nature revealed by this record, more than merely a "reasonable relation to some purpose within the competency of the State" is required* to sustain the validity of the State's requirement under the First Amendment. To be sure, the power of the parent, even when linked to a free exercise claim, may be subject to limitation under *Prince* if it appears that parental decisions will jeopardize the health and safety of the child, or have a potential for significant social burdens. But in this case, the Amish have introduced persuasive evidence undermining the arguments the State has advanced to

---

[48]*Wisconsin v. Yoder*, 406 U.S. 205, 215 (1972); see also *Cantwell v. Connecticut*, 310 U.S. 296, 307-308 (1940).

[49]406 U.S., at 232.

support its claims in terms of the welfare of the child and society as a whole.[50]

Eighteen states require some form of state approval for private, religious schools, but only Iowa, North Dakota, and Michigan "still require both state approval of church schools and certification of their teachers."[51] The controversy with respect to such laws involves the question of whether the parent or the State is the primary educator. And the essential claim of the religious schools, the parents, and their children is not merely educational, but primarily religious.

---

[50]406 U.S., at 233-234 (emphasis added).
[51]N.Y. Times, March 25, 1987, p. 1, col. 2.

Classroom Sex Education: Undermining Parental Rights

James Likoudis

Author's note: The following reflections focus on the phenomenon of classroom-curriculum sex education as it has functioned in both public and parochial schools. They are written as a commentary on Pope John Paul II's repeated affirmation of the primacy of parental rights in education and the centrality of the family in social life and organization.

> Sex education, which is a basic right and duty of parents, must always be carried out under their attentive guidance whether at home or in educational centers chosen and controlled by them. In this regard, the Church reaffirms the law of subsidiarity, which the school is bound to observe when it cooperates in sex education, by entering into the same spirit which animates the parents.
>
> — *Familiaris Consortio*, 37

> Those in society who are in charge of schools must never forget that the parents have been appointed by God himself as the first and principal educators of their children and that their right is completely inalienable.
>
> — *Familiaris Consortio*, 40

From time to time, the question of sex education, especially as regards programs being used in schools, becomes a matter of concern to Catholic parents. The principles concerning this have been sufficiently, but clearly, enunciated in *Familiaris Consortio*. First among these

principles is the need to recognize that sex education is a
basic right and duty of parents themselves. They have to be
helped to become increasingly more effective in fulfilling
this task. Other educational agencies have an important
role, BUT ALWAYS IN A SUBSIDIARY MANNER,
WITH DUE SUBORDINATION TO THE RIGHTS OF
PARENTS.

— Pope John Paul II
Address to the U.S. Bishops, No. 19
September 16, 1987

◆

There is no area in American education where parental
rights and the moral values upholding traditional family life have
been more ignored, derided, and violated than in the area of sex
education, *which has become part of the curriculum* in many public
and parochial schools. For two decades, *classroom sex education
in mixed groups* has been the chosen vehicle whereby a permissive
philosophy of sex (fostered by leading secular humanists in
American society) has been popularized among the general
public. *Classroom-curriculum sex education* has been an
essentially *elitist* and *totalitarian* movement. It has resulted in not
only a serious erosion of parental authority in our society but also
the loss of parental control over school systems and the spread of
sexual immorality among youth exposed to the *amoral* ("values-
neutral") sex education programs that have proliferated the last
twenty years. Statistics are plentiful regarding the increase in
every index of sexual delinquency among American youth, but
not enough attention has been paid to the impact of the amoral
programs of sex education directed at the young in our public
schools (where "education in human sexuality" has been
deliberately divorced from traditional moral teaching rooted in
classical Natural Law and the Judaeo-Christian ethic). The

radical innovation of *classroom-curriculum sex education* has reaped a bitter harvest. As the U.S. Secretary of Education, William J. Bennett, recently wrote:

> In all too many places, sex education classes are failing to give the American people what they are entitled to expect for their children, and what their children deserve.
>
> Seventy percent of all high school seniors had taken sex education courses in 1985, up from 60 percent in 1976. Yet when we look at what is happening in the sexual lives of American students, we can only conclude that it is doubtful that much sex education is doing any good at all. The statistics by which we may measure how our children — how our boys and girls — are treating one another sexually are little short of staggering:
>
> — More than one half of American young people have had sexual intercourse by the time they are 17.
> — More than one million teen-age girls in the United States become pregnant each year. Of those who give birth, nearly half are not yet 18.
> — Teen pregnancy rates are at or near an all-time high. A 25-percent decline in birth rates between 1970 and 1984 is due to a doubling of the abortion rate during that period. More than 400,000 teen-age girls now have abortions each year.
> — Unwed teen-age childbirths rose 200 percent between 1960 and 1980.
> — Forty percent of today's 14-year old girls will become pregnant by the time they are 19.
>
> These numbers are, I believe, an irrefutable indictment of sex education's effectiveness in reducing teen-age sexual activity and pregnancies. For these numbers have grown even as sex education has expanded. I do not suggest that sex education has caused the increase in sexual activity among youth; but clearly it has not prevented it.[1]

---

[1]William J. Bennett, "Sex and the Education of Our Children," *America* (February 14, 1987), pp. 120-121.

It would doubtless be an exaggeration to say that school sex education programs have been the only cause of the sexual activity among youth in our society (resulting in more fornication, more adultery, more homosexuality, more contraception, more abortion, more child molestation and pedophilia, more pornography, and over 20 new venereal diseases including the terminal disease of AIDS). There have been *other* factors at work affecting people's "life-style" and their view of sexual morality. America's porno culture, a TV media geared to endless sexual titillation and commercial exploitation, the sophisticated contempt for the traditional moral values of Western Civilization indulged in by deracinated liberal intelligentsia in our universities and colleges, and the "sexual politics" networking pursued by ultra-liberal organizations (e.g., the National Education Association, People for the American Way, the National Parents-Teachers Association, The American Civil Liberties Union, the Sex Information and Education Council of the United States, Planned Parenthood, etc.) all have been powerful agents dissolving the Classical-Christian understanding of moral norms regulating sexual behavior. As Secretary Bennett went on to observe:

> In too many of our schools . . . the words of morality, of a rational, mature morality, seem to have been banished from this sort of sex education. . . . Apparently being "comfortable" with one's decision is the only consensual value left.[2]

Interestingly, since the beginning of public education in the early 1800's, and except for a brief period after World War I, it was rarely thought that sex education was an area of competence for public school authorities and their government schools. The best educators cherishing the Liberal Arts tradition of the West had always thought that sex education (being a facet of the *religious and moral education* of the child) could not be effectively

---

[2]*Ibid.*, pp. 122-123.

taught by means of a formal course in the curriculum of a public school soon presuming to be "religiously neutral." Then, too, the most respectable educators, psychologists, and moralists (those, at any rate, interested in the mental and emotional health of children and in their souls' welfare) had expressed the most serious reservations about the spectacle of boys and girls discussing sexual matters without any firm moral guidance — and at the crass invasion of privacy such instruction inevitably involves. Moreover, many parents had looked askance at the use of tax monies to impose a *sex education program without morality* on all students. From a traditional moral point of view, *sex education without morality* had been regarded as a pedagogical horror — the product of dehumanized and soul-less bureaucrats who, in gnostic fashion, thought select bits of "knowledge" called "education" would automatically solve all problems. In our own day, Alexander Solzhenitsyn, rightly regarded as a fearless prophet denouncing contemporary moral evils, has commented at length concerning the materialistic humanism rotting the moral fiber of the West. A thoroughly documented study of the decadent sex education in progress in the schools of our nation (whether public, private, or parochial) could only conclude that a materialistic humanism is clearly reflected in the sex education programs in place (and enjoying the support of a massive media propaganda which has duped millions of parents). Other more discerning parents were to be left helpless before a Sex Education Juggernaut that would trample their parental rights into the dust. As a result of sex education programs introduced into the curriculum of the schools of the nation (under the guise of "assisting or complementing" the parents), millions of youth have been inculcated in purely secular (and materialistic) values concerning sexuality, being as misled as surely as Soviet youth were in having all morality severed from religious values. Even today, it is doubtful that a large majority of the legislators who fund public education or the school board members responsible for the educational offerings in their local school districts, have fully grasped the oddity of classroom-curriculum sex education as desirable educational pedagogy. Nor have they assessed classroom-curriculum sex education being intrinsically bound up with the "New Morality" of the Sexual Revolution and constituting, in itself, to quote Dr. Russell Kirk, "a pseudo-religion, hostile to Christianity, Judaism, and the Perennial Philosophy."[3]

The role played by leading secular humanists in helping to entrench sex education in the schools cannot be stressed sufficiently. It is in the area of *sexual morality* that secular humanists (remarkably active in the liberal societies of the West) have prided themselves on the "progress" they have made. As they themselves have put it: "Humanists have had an important role in the sexual revolution." In the January/February 1976 issue of *The Humanist*, Dr. Paul Kurtz published "A New Bill of Sexual Rights and Responsibilities" which starkly revealed the secular humanist assault on traditional Judaeo-Christian sexual morality [though war had already been declared in *Humanist Manifesto I* (1933) and *Humanist Manifesto II* (1973)]. "A New Bill of Sexual Rights and Responsibilities" clarified what secular humanists meant by the "morality" they intended to promote through "moral education" in the public schools. Such "moral education" (translated: classroom sex education) was endorsed, Dr. Kurtz noted, by "humanist authors in the forefront of humanistic sexology." The "New Bill" was full of the most sophisticated (and deceptive) rhetoric concerning "meaningful human relationships" and the "humanization of morality," and assumed the most elevated moral tone. But it is not too much to say that it gave the Imprimatur of contemporary American secular humanism to the detailed agenda of the nation's most permissive sexologists. The following were given explicit sanction: fornication, adultery,

---

[3]Dr. Russell Kirk, "Schools and Moral Instruction," *National Review* (July 29, 1969), p. 752.

contraception, abortion, masturbation, homosexuality and lesbianism, and pornography.

For example, masturbation was declared to be "a viable mode of satisfaction for many individuals, young and old, and should be fully accepted." Traditional Jewish and Christian moral restrictions on sexual behavior were relegated to the status of "repressive and archaic taboos" and any effort to regulate the most aberrant consequences of sexual delinquency by legislative enactments were declared "intolerable." "Forms of sexual expression should not be a matter of legal regulation." The signers of the "New Bill" (many of them holding prestigious academic chairs in the sciences) rhapsodized as follows concerning their philosophy of sexual liberation:

> At this point in our history, we human beings are embarking on a wondrous adventure. For the first time we realize that we own our own bodies. Until now our bodies have been in bondage to church or state, which have dictated how we could express our sexuality. We have not been permitted to experience the pleasure and the joy of the human body and our sensory nature to their full capacity.[4]

The entire document makes for interesting reading in hindsight and in light of today's AIDS epidemic and the desperate effort now to justify *condom-education* in the schools. Its profound animus against organized religion (especially the Catholic Church) and the biblical ethic was similarly reflected in yet another Humanist production, *A Secular Humanist Declaration* (published in 1980), which also decried the Classical and Judaeo-Christian tradition of civility and decency. For all the posturing about "values" characterizing the various secular humanist Manifestoes and Declarations, in the last analysis they cannot be said to sanction *objective values*; they rather revel in the

---

[4]See the full text of "A New Bill of Sexual Rights and Responsibilities" signed by Lester Kirkendall and other leading sexologists in *The Humanist*, (January/February 1976).

subjectivist effusions which satisfy a decadent secular liberal intelligentsia. Their bias against "indoctrination" masks an absolutist mentality opposed to the realistic metaphysics of the Perennial Philosophy as well as to the modern relevance of biblical ethics. Their *Manifestoes* reveal the most servile adherence to the moral relativism embodied in Situation Ethics.

This contemporary assault on man's intrinsic dignity (stemming from modern secular liberalism's denial of God and the creation of man in His image and likeness) was to receive immense reinforcement in the faddist classroom sex education uncritically introduced into the nation's schools. Contrary to the prevailing myths surrounding sex education, the schools have been part of the Sexual Revolution, rather than any solution to the latter's debilitating effects on the moral fiber of Western societies.[5] Schools furthering moral and sexual permissiveness have contributed directly to the ethical anarchy already far advanced in our own country — with sad consequences for the intrinsic dignity of the individual, the welfare of the family, the role of parental authority, and the common good of society (where a proper balance between the family and the school should be displayed). Classroom sex education has introduced a further note of collectivism into education as liberal legislators, school officials, and professional educators and teachers proceed to crush the opposition of parents to the children's sexual liberation movement being fostered by permissive schools. It has been traditional religious parents (Catholic, Protestant, and Jew) who have been particularly conscious of the secular humanist animus permeating sex education in the schools. They were to quickly discover that classroom sex education, Values Clarification, techniques of Sensitivity Training, and other curriculum courses focusing on inter-personal relationships and the use of group dynamics — geared to encouraging the creation

---

[5]See James Likoudis, "The Mythology of Modern Sex Education," *Social Justice Review* (March-April 1982), pp. 45-50.

of the "morally autonomous" student (i.e., one whose personal freedom in making moral choices is so emphasized, exaggerated, and extolled) — not only lacked conformity to traditional religious and moral teaching but were divorced from any objective moral order. They were to sense that, in sex education and other humanistic exercises, their children were being exposed to a progressive liberation from the natural order of things (as known by sound metaphysics, rigorous reasoning, or common sense) and were being led to view their parents, churches, and synagogues as oppressive instruments of an antiquated "conventional morality." From 1965 into the '80s, an increasing number of parents would be confronted by their pre-teens and adolescents with the familiar refrains: "This may be true or right for you, but not for me," and "Who are you to impose your morality on me?" A parental moral code grounded in the Ten commandments would be confronted with the "open, flexible, non-judgmental" value-system of "democratic pluralism." Parents carefully examining the classroom-curriculum sex education being offered in their public schools would soon have no doubt that the structure, content, and methodology of school sex education had been designed by its ideological advocates as their instrument for entrenching the contraceptive-abortion mentality in American society.

No brief article can do justice to the sufferings of parents caught up in the ugly sex education controversies that have erupted in public school districts (and also in parochial schools) across the nation. These controversies continue today in both the public and parochial school sectors in the U.S. (and also, it may be added, in Canada) as parents have struggled to have input into curriculum sex education offerings and to safeguard their parental rights in education. They have attempted to protect their adolescents from a subtle (and sometimes not so subtle) indoctrination in secular humanism and to safeguard their younger children from objectionable and offensive sexually explicit materials (texts, films, records, recommended reading materials) making a mockery of the virtues of chastity and modesty. The more conscientious parents did battle with school boards and professional educators intent on implementing one of the key planks of collectivistic liberalism's agenda for "educational reform." Receiving little support from a generally hostile media, parental wrath has not been sufficient to dislodge most sex education programs (often sneaked into school districts' offerings by a pattern of lying and deception unprecedented in the annals of American education). School officials often denied the existence of sex education in their schools despite documented evidence to the contrary; others engaged in deliberate misinformation concerning legislative "mandating" of sex education (when there was no such "mandate"). The disinformation accompanying the propaganda for classroom sex education was extended to the coining of the now-standard euphemisms adorning curriculum manuals for "Family Life Education" or "Human Growth and Development" or "Growth Patterns and Character Education."

The Sex Information and Education Council's (SIECUS) masterful technician, Dr. Lester Kirkendall (the main author, incidentally, of the aforementioned "New Bill of Sexual Rights and Responsibilities") revealed his own grasp of the consummate art of dissembling at a hush-hush session of fellow sexologists meeting in the Anaheim Charter House Hotel in December 1968. After labelling adversaries of sex education programs "a fringe group of dissenters who don't think rationally" and declaring that "society is changing, and the basis for authority has shifted from the religious to the secular," he disclosed SIECUS's recipe for success in dealing with parental opposition to a school district's sex program:

> Just sneak it in as an experimental course and see how people react. Go to your PTA and get support. That's where the power lies. Don't say that you are going to start a sex education course. Always move forward. Say that you are going to enrich, expand and make it better. The

opposition can't stop something that you have already started.[6]

A major obstacle was placed before the Sex Education Juggernaut, however, in 1969 when New York State parents and parent groups were able to prevent a legislative *mandating* of sex education. In 1967, Governor Nelson Rockefeller had signed "without comment" a New York State Health Law *eliminating* the fateful words: "nutrition, *mental and emotional health, family living*, disease prevention and control and accident prevention."[7] However, for the previous three years, various school board members, administrators, and Education Department officials had pressured and stampeded local school districts to prepare curricula and teachers for a prospective "mandated" program of sex education. State Senator Edmund J. Speno, chief architect of the 1967 New York State Health Law and recipient of a torrent of protests from all parts of the state, reacted strongly to the bureaucratic chicanery and deception engaged in by education officials. In a letter to Mr. James E. Allen, the New York State Commissioner of Education and a militant promoter of classroom sex education, Senator Speno wrote:

> As author of the law, I was careful to limit the mandate for curriculum change to the limited areas of critical health problems caused by the habituation to smoking, drugs and alcoholism. In the past several weeks it has been brought to my attention by virtually hundreds of letters, telephone calls and inquiries from my colleagues in the Legislature, that your Department is attempting to develop a sex education program in our educational system and is relying on the critical health problems law as the basis for developing this new subject matter in the schools.
> At the time the law was drafted your Department recommended that I include sex education in the law and I

---

[6]Quoted in *Anaheim Bulletin* (Anaheim, Calif.), December 18, 19, 20, 1968 by Staff Writer John Steimbacher.

[7]"Rocky Signs New Law for Health Education — Sex Not Mentioned," *Buffalo Evening News* (May 26, 1969).

specifically rejected the recommendation because I felt that it would be improper for the Legislature to mandate a course of study concerning such a sensitive and personal area of interest.

It has also come to my attention that your Department may very well be relying on funds appropriated for the specific subject matters of the critical health problems to develop curriculum materials in sex education. You will note from the attached letter which I have sent to the members of the Legislature that the law which I have sponsored in no way mandates a course of study in sex education (Letter of March 28, 1969 — released to the press).

Nevertheless, frustrated in its frenetic effort to impose classroom sex education by a state-wide legislative mandate, the New York State Education Department proceeded to engage in a concentrated campaign to induce and "persuade" local districts to establish "pilot programs" of sex education and encourage their establishment on a "local community basis." Such programs would initiate a new "comprehensive health curriculum" (wherein "personality development," human sexuality, and family life education would be adroitly subsumed under "Mental Health Education"). Progressive liberals in other states would follow a similar pattern of pressing for a "comprehensive health curriculum" in their school districts on a state-wide compulsory or local voluntary basis.

The result of such efforts is the present situation of widespread classroom sex education divorced from the traditional moral norms of the Classical Western Tradition and now entrenched in many states. *Time* magazine has recently noted:

> About 80% of public school children in major U.S. cities now take some kind of sex education course. As for national figures, no one knows for sure: sex education is strictly a local matter, varying widely from one community to the next, and few accurate statistics are kept. Only

Maryland, New Jersey, and Washington D.C. require the subject in all schools.[8]

Despite the obvious failure of classroom sex education programs to enforce sexual restraint (the argument educationists had used originally to persuade parents of the utility of such "education"), this has not daunted the fanatic efforts of die-hard proponents. The same issue of *Time* quotes a "sex education consultant" to a school district as chortling: "Under 15% of U.S. children get really good sex education. We are only beginning to institute adequate programs."[9] Presently, Planned Parenthood and other groups pressing for "comprehensive programs in human sexuality" are attempting to take advantage of public concern over AIDS to lobby diligently for public funds to establish School-Based Health Clinics in public schools (which will dispense condoms and other contraceptives to students). An especially ominous development is the attempt to disarm "conservative critics" of classroom sex education by taking advantage of the popular fervor to revitalize for youth the ideals of abstinence and chastity, thereby pressuring more parents "to accept sex instruction in the schools."[10]

As a Catholic Bishop was to observe some years ago, many religiously-oriented parents have reacted strongly to the teaching of *moral relativism* enshrined in public school sex education programs. A remarkable loss of confidence in public schooling for the latter's academic and moral failures has led hundreds of thousands of Catholic and evangelical fundamentalist Protestant parents to withdraw their children from the public schools. Many new private or independent lay schools have been established by parents banding together; many parents even began to engage in home-schooling their children taking advantage of the more

---

[8]John Leo, "Sex Education: What Should Children Know? When Should They Know It?," *Time* (November 24, 1986), p. 55.

[9]*Ibid.*, p. 55.

[10]*Ibid.*, p. 63.

lenient education laws in their states. (Other parents doing home-schooling would be accused of violating the compulsory education laws of their states, taken to court for child neglect or child abuse by school officials, or harassed in other ways). Interestingly, there has been a significant loss of confidence by many Catholic parents in the Church's parochial schools. A large exodus of parents from Catholic parochial and diocesan high schools witnesses to disaffection with Catholic schools being caused by the same disastrous trends that have destroyed the quality of education in public schools.

> There is also a moral relativism, an erosion of authority and a blurring of sexual identity evident in Catholic education in our day. This is what the Holy See has referred to as the "Crisis of Faith" in the Church — because in some quarters there has been a serious loss of confidence in the basics of Catholic doctrine. This but illustrates how effectual the program of moral relativism in the public schools has been.[11]

Here, again, formal classroom sex instruction (offensively *clinical* in nature) can be identified as a major reason for many Catholic parents abandoning the parochial school system. As one Catholic mother has eloquently observed (and her voice is legion):

> Sex educators have preached so continuously about parents' lapse of duty in this area that they have created a whole generation of head-hanging, breast-beating, guilt-ridden parents and clergy! The implication, of course, is that we have all been failures! And the result is that we have allowed millions of our very young children to be led into early sexual activity (fornication), by neutralizing sex and placing it in a laboratory atmosphere.
> Our children in parochial schools now have classes in which the children must discuss the mechanics of sex; such as learn what sexual desire is and how it causes erections in

---

[11]Bishop Thomas V. Dolinay, "Editorial," *Eastern Catholic Life*, (July 25, 1982), p. 4.

the male and mucous discharge in the female. This to children from 11-14 years of age! They learn where the sperm originates and how it is released into the female. And how it travels from the vagina through the different sexual organs. They discuss homosexuality; some children know nothing about it, some a great deal.

They discuss masturbation, what it is and how it is done; some children are still innocent. They discuss venereal disease, sexual fantasies, etc! This is criminal in children who haven't even gone through puberty. These children are 9, 10, 11, 12, 13, and 14.

What happened to privacy? Our poor children are forced under penalty of being ridiculed by teachers and peers to participate in discussions and questionnaires strictly against their instinctive sense of privacy and holy shame (modesty). This is another principle that the say-all, know-all sex educators cannot understand: They do not believe in the God-given authority of parents united with God in the Sacrament of Marriage; such parents are better qualified to teach their own children. Nor do these sex educators understand the Scriptures concerning man's fallen nature and inclination toward evil. And the parents, having been made to feel inadequate, tolerate this. God forgive them.[12]

The above represents the kind of strong response made by Catholic parents to the classroom sex education programs that have won their way into Catholic elementary schools: the Chicago *Becoming a Person* program; the *Benziger Family Life* program; the Rochester *Education in Love* program; the *Sadlier Look at Life* program; and the William C. Brown Co.'s *New Creation* series even led to the unusual intervention by Edouard Cardinal Gagnon, president of the Vatican's Pontifical Council for the Family, who labelled *New Creation* "a travesty of sex education." The Vatican's concern to defend the family unit against the growing statism and totalitarianism evident in the modern educational schemes of Western liberal democratic states, Third World socialist states, and Eastern bloc

---

[12]Ruth Johnson, "Letter to the Editor," *Homiletic and Pastoral Review* (December 1984), p. 9.

dictatorships, has led, interestingly, to the Holy See's issuing a remarkable document entitled *Charter on the Rights of the Family* (November 24, 1983 — and published in response to a call by the 1980 World Synod of Bishops meeting in Rome). The following excerpts bear on the problems posed by classroom sex education in many countries:

— The family, a natural society, exists prior to the state or any other community and possesses rights which are inalienable. (Preamble)

— Since they have conferred life on their children, parents have the original, primary and inalienable right to educate them; hence they must be acknowledged as the first and foremost educators of their children. (Art. 5)

— Parents have the right to educate their children in conformity with their moral and religious convictions. (Art. 5.a.)

— Parents have the right to choose freely schools or other means necessary to educate their children in keeping with their convictions. (Art. 5.b.)

— Parents have the right to insure that their children are not compelled to attend classes which are not in agreement with their own moral and religious convictions. In particular, sex education is a basic right of the parents and must always be carried out under their close supervision, whether at home or in educational centers chosen and controlled by them. (Art. 5.c.)

— The primary right of parents to educate their children must be upheld in all forms of collaboration between parents, teachers and school authorities. (Art. 5.c.)

— Parents have the right to form associations with other families and institutions, in order to fulfill the family's role suitably and effectively, as well as to protect the rights, foster the good and represent the interests of the family. (Art. 8.a.)

Despite the protests of those parents regarding classroom sex education as "morally objectionable" and the efforts of concerned parents and parental groups to dislodge or remove such programs from their schools (whether public or parochial), there has been the general failure of the legal community to safeguard effectively the rights of parents in sex education. From the days of the famous Gracey case in the late 1960's (when 6 of the 9 children of Mr. and Mrs. Gerald Gracey of Mexico, N.Y., were seized by sheriff's deputies and taken from the parents' custody for their non-attendance at the school's contraceptive sex education classes), parents have seen their children subjected to the most appalling "instruction" violating their personal, moral and/or religious convictions. Parents have sometimes been refused *exemption* of their children from classes regarded as objectionable and offensive. They have seen their children ostracized and discriminated against, and mocked and ridiculed (and sometimes suffering spiritual, mental and emotional injury) for their parents' firm resistance to classroom sex instruction. Parents themselves have been subjected to harassment and vindictive treatment by school board members, teachers and sycophants of the local PTA or Home-School Association. Protesting parents in parochial schools have been told: "If you don't like it, get out!" (which many, indeed, have proceeded to do). Legal suits to remove offending course programs, texts, audio-visual aids, and subject material (ranging from tasteless descriptions of sexual intercourse to the holding of rap sessions on anal and oral sex to the dispensing of information on how to masturbate, use condoms and the pill, and obtain an abortion, etc.) have been stymied by parental unwillingness to cause their children more emotional suffering and lawyers' failure to provide the necessary legal grounds (for parental suits) drawn from constitutional and education law. Parents' efforts to have recourse to legal procedures have also been hampered by lack of funds to pursue costly and timely lawsuits. There has also been a lack of parental organization necessary to pursue legislative changes on the federal and state levels which would cripple the privacy-invading thrust intrinsic to classroom sex education. The one promising tool available to parents (the so-called Hatch Amendment or Hatch Protection of Pupil Rights Amendment passed unanimously by the U.S. Senate in 1978) has proved useless since the U.S. Education Department has yet to issue enforcement regulations. The text of the Hatch Amendment is worth the study of attorneys seeking to redress the grievances of parents with regards to classroom sex instruction by exploring the possibilities of more effective legislation on both the federal and state levels:

Protection of Pupil Rights

Sec. 1250. Section 439 of the General Education Provisions Act, 20 USC 1232 h. (relating to protection of pupil rights) is amended by inserting "(a)" after "439" and by adding at the end thereof a new subsection as follows:

(b) No student shall be required, as part of any applicable program, to submit to psychiatric examination, testing, or treatment, or psychological examination, testing, or treatment, in which the primary purpose is to reveal information concerning:

    (1)   political affiliations;

    (2)   mental and psychological problems potentially embarrassing to the student or his family;

    (3)   sex behavior and attitudes;

    (4)   illegal, anti-social, self-incriminating and demeaning behavior;

    (5)   critical appraisals of other individuals with whom respondents have close family relationships;

    (6)   legally recognized privileged and analogous relationships, such as those of lawyers, physicians, and ministers; or

    (7)   income (other than that required by law to determine eligibility for participation in a program or for

receiving financial assistance under such program), without the prior consent of the student (if the student is an adult or emancipated minor), or in the case of unemancipated minor, without the prior written consent of the parent.

(20 USC 123h) Enacted November 2, 1978, P.L. 95-561.

(The Education Amendments of 1978, Enacted November 2, 1978)

Though the *Hatch Amendment* represented something of a victory for parental efforts, it has proved of little practical benefit in view of its remaining an unenforceable piece of federal legislation. Moreover, legal suits to stop the assault on traditional moral and family values embodied in classroom sex instruction on grounds that such "education" involves actual indoctrination in the "religion of Secular Humanism" [cf. *Torcaso v. Watkins*, 367 U.S. 488 (1961)] have met with disbelief and hostility from judges wedded to secular liberal ideology.

In 1972, the Supreme Court of the United States declared:

The values of parental direction of the religious upbringing and education of their children in their early and formative years have a high place in our society. . . . Thus a state's interest in universal education, however highly we rank it, is not totally free from a balancing process when it impinges on fundamental rights and interests, such as those specifically protected by the Free Exercise Clause of the First Amendment, and the traditional interest of parents with respect to the religious upbringing of their children so long as they, in the words of *Pierce v. Society of Sisters* (1925) "prepare them for additional obligations" (pp. 213-214).

The history and culture of Western civilization reflect a strong tradition of parental concern for the nurture and upbringing of their children. This primary role of the parents in the upbringing of their children is now established beyond debate as an enduring American Tradition.

[*Wisconsin v. Yoder*, 406 U.S. 205 (1972)]

If the above is true, it might be suggested that a ringing affirmation of parental rights in the matter of their minors seeking an abortion (and a reversal of the 1973 *Roe v. Wade* decision) is assuredly in order. Again, *a fortiori*, if parental rights are due to be given more than lip service in American society and education, then the disturbing phenomenon of classroom sex instruction (with all its ideological overtones) must be seen for what it is:

— a conspicuous violation and usurpation of what Americans have traditionally considered the primary educational rights of parents;

— a gross intrusion upon the personal privacy and dignity of both children and parents, resulting in the disturbance of the ordinary rhythms of family life;

— a menace to the spiritual and emotional welfare of youth because of its excessive biological focus on genital sexuality;

— a collectivistic basic attack on human dignity with its undermining of the legitimate independence, stability, and integrity of the family;

— an unwarranted extension of the power of government in the public school sector with its intervention into the most delicate and sensitive area of people's lives.

— a fertile source of moral corruption in the body politic as both parental authority and the sexual morality of youth are undermined by governmental favor shown educators engaged in a neo-pagan assault on traditional Judaeo-Christian values and morals.

It is not sufficient that legal measures be enacted to protect parental rights by allowing parents to exempt their children from classroom sex instruction involving values and judgments and/or attitudes concerning human reproduction, sexual promiscuity, methods of contraception and abortion, and sexual perversion — all matters which many parents find personally reprehensible.

Such exemption from certain classes is rendered impossible in some public and parochial schools where *classroom sex instruction is integrated throughout the curriculum.* Legal exemption does not, moreover, prevent the ugly discrimination and ostracism of non-participating students which often takes place. It is certainly curious to observe that whereas public prayer has been effectively removed from public schools on the grounds of discrimination against non-participating students, our courts refuse to draw a similar conclusion with regards to the equally sensitive area of classroom sex instruction.

The obligation to adequately safeguard the rights of parents in the general area of education and, specifically, in the crucial area of sex education is one of the great needs and tasks of our day. It is to be hoped that attorneys and jurists will assist parents in putting real teeth into the concept of "the primacy of parental rights in education" and collaborate with parental, civic, and church organizations seeking legal protections for children and youth from injurious educational fads and experiments which are substituted for real learning.

Information concerning the organization Mr. Likoudis heads, Catholics United for the Faith (CUF), and its materials evaluating sex education programs in both public and parochial schools is available by writing:

CUF
45 Union Avenue
New Rochelle, NY 10801
(914) 235-9404

State Intervention in the Family and Parental Rights: A Psychological Assessment

Roger Rinn

The changes in our society over the past quarter century have been staggering. The problems which parents face as a result of these changes are, for many, overwhelming. consider the following list as a partial accounting:

1. The sexual revolution with rampant infectious diseases (some of which are incurable) and high rates of pregnancies and births among unwed teens;

2. The chronic, alarming rates of accidents and resultant deaths from teenaged drivers under the influence of alcohol and other drugs;

3. The persistent use and abuse of chemical substances by adolescents; and

4. The incredibly high rate of juvenile crime (as compared with adult crime) and relatively light legal consequences to the juvenile offender.

Couple these considerations with the current societal emphasis on children's rights (as opposed to parents' rights) and it is not difficult to understand why many parents have thrown in the towel and abdicated their responsibilities as "caregivers" of their offspring.   Indeed, helplessness is a constant theme among countless parents of teenagers.

My views regarding parental rights are based on the assumption that those aspects of legislation which deprive parents of influence with their children tend to weaken the family, transferring control and responsibility for childrearing to the state.

This paper will address the issue of parental rights from my perspective as a psychologist in clinical practice. It is my belief that emphasis on such rights offers hope for troubled families. I will not review the vast literature on behaviorally disordered youth.   Rather, I will describe my theoretical bias on the functioning of families in terms of behavior acquisition and change and then interject practical implications where appropriate.

What are Parents' Rights?

It is my impression that parents have become secondary in interest and focus over the past half century. However, many persist in the belief that they as parents have certain rights which must be enforceable in order to rear normal, moral children. A partial list follows:

1. Parents have the right to be treated with respect by their children and other caregivers (e.g., teachers, probation officers). Children who are disrespectful engage in yelling and arguing, anger, sarcasm, hostile tone of voice, hitting, swearing, and talking back;

2. Parents have the right to have their requests adhered to by their children (i.e., compliance) in a timely fashion;

3. Parents have the right to have their children behave in a manner consonant with parental beliefs (morality, achievement, health, and manners);

4. Parents have the right to expect children to live within the legal boundaries of society; and

5. Parents have the right to be informed and take part in any extra-familial activities or problems of their children.

With these rights go many more responsibilities. Respect for parents must be balanced with respect for children. Let me be perfectly clear: I am opposed to corporal punishment of children (I propose that we save it for adult offenders with histories of violent crime). Parents must develop contingency management skills and approach behavior problems with "kind firmness." Later in this paper, I will integrate upon children's behaviors.

Theoretical Framework

In order to make inferences about the effects of legislative actions upon families, a theoretical explanation of family functioning and its effects on children's behaviors is necessary. My theoretical preference is that of social learning theory. Applied social learning theory assumes that behavior is learned in the social context of family, peer group, and community living, among others. Moreover, behavior is a function of antecedent and consequent events.

The most outstanding proponent of social learning theory is, in my opinion, Gerald R. Patterson, a gifted and creative research psychologist. With impressive empirical support, Patterson and his colleagues have demonstrated the relationship between family behavior and children's behavior.[1] A succinct statement of his conceptualization and empirical findings has been presented by Wells:

> As a performance theory, coercion theory first attempts to describe the characteristics of aggressive children which

---

[1]Patterson (1982).

differentiate them from normal children. Early in his research program, Patterson found that most aggressive children began their careers with the same aversive behaviors displayed by normal children (e.g., whining, yelling, noncompliance, teasing, hitting, etc.). Furthermore, these behaviors often were displayed in the context of interactions with other people and often occurred in "bursts." What characterized the aggressive child was the frequency and duration of these chains or bursts of aversive social interaction. Aggressive children displayed more frequent chains and chains of longer duration. Their aversive behaviors were not random, but contingent; that is, they were more likely to occur in the presence of specific behaviors from other family members. Furthermore, the child's aversive behaviors were used contingently to produce a reliable impact on the victim (i.e., to control his/her behavior). The victims' reactions, in turn, appeared to have short- and long-term effects on the child aggressor. The short-term effect was an increase in the duration of the immediate interaction. The long-term effect was to increase the likelihood of future aggression, or what Patterson refers to as the disposition to behave aggressively.

It is this process of "pain control" that is the fundamental building block of Patterson's coercion theory. In this process, the reactions of the aggressive child's victims contribute substantially to his aggression performance level. Therefore, a partial answer to the question of what causes aggressive children to behave the way they do is to be found in the behavior of other persons.[2]

In essence, social learning theory postulates the potent effects of parental and sibling actions as developers and perpetuators of deviant behaviors in children. Forces external to the family likewise direct and control children's behaviors, e.g., peers, schools, media, and the legal system, becoming more influential as the child passes puberty. When adequate opportunities and rewards for pro-social behaviors are not

---

[2]Wells (1984), pp. 122-123.

forthcoming and punishment is incompetently administered, deviant behaviors persist.

Genetics undoubtedly plays a role in the development of a child's behavioral repertoire. Children are born with differing intellectual capacities and activity levels, to name only two. Even the most radical behaviorist will privately (and, sometimes, publicly) admit this. However, we are "stuck" with our genes and have no technique for altering them to obtain a desired behavior effect. Therefore, hereditary factors notwithstanding, social learning theory along with its applications is a most useful conceptual tool with which to view the law's effects upon families. Patterson and numerous other researchers have provided evidence supporting the theory.

Parents' Rights and Children's Behavior

If parental rights are indeed related to children's behaviors, then any governmental action which affects such rights likewise affects children's behavioral repertoires. I contend that such a relationship exists and is potent.

When parents are maligned by teachers or probation officers (and others such as psychologists, etc.), children frequently follow suit. Needless to say, children have an uncanny ability to strike at a parent's weakest area. The last thing we need is more aggressive criticism aimed at parents and heard by children. Legislation which detracts from parental rights of respect and compliance also detracts from pro-social behavior by children. *If children don't have to be respectful of parents and compliant to their wishes, they grow like weeds in all directions, devoid of substance and character.* From social learning theory we know that parents *must* be able to administer consequences calmly and consistently. If the courts will not or cannot assist in the endeavor, parents are literally "out on a limb."

The secret nature of many types of interaction between teens and governmental agencies or other caregivers (e.g., mental health professionals) clearly makes it impossible for parents to enter into decision-making with their children. How can a parent provide appropriate consequences for undesirable behavior if these behaviors are hidden and covered up by others (who may tacitly approve)?

If one accepts the rights of parents as givers, then tampering with them is tantamount to altering the nature of the family. Great care must be taken when legislating to correct an evil because another may be created, or the first may actually be made worse.

Effects of Governmental Action

The influence of legislative action on families will now be considered. I have selected three areas as targets which have impacted my patients' families: juvenile justice, family planning, and the legal drinking age.

Juvenile Justice

In order to grasp the magnitude of juvenile crime in the country, consider the following:

1. "Persons under the age of 18 are responsible for 45 percent of all arrests for serious crime and for 23 percent of all arrests for violent crime"[3];

2. "Between 1970 and 1977 the adult arrest rate for index crimes (e.g., murder, burglary) increased by 21 percent and the juvenile rate by 22 percent, but the arrest rate for juveniles has remained approximately 65 percent greater than that for adults"[4];

---

[3]U.S. Department of Justice (1976), p. 1.
[4]Weis and Hawkins (1979), p. 1.

3. ". . . of the total arrests for index violence, juveniles account for 44 percent of them while adults account for 56 percent"[5]; and

4. "The peak age for arrests for violent crimes is 18, followed by 17, 16, and 19. The peak age for arrests for major property crimes is 16, followed by 15 and 17."[6]

There is ample evidence indicating that many of the youngsters who committed these crimes preceded their violent activities by less serious offenses including so called "status" offenses (e.g., ungovernable behavior, truancy, running away from home). It may be assumed that treatment of status offenders would decrease the probability of violent crime at a later time.

The Department of Justice has referred to the increase in juvenile crime as the "crisis in delinquency" and rightly so.[7] Taking into consideration the frightening statistics and what was said regarding status offenses, Congress, in 1974, enacted the Juvenile Justice and Delinquency Prevention Act to combat the problem. The Act called for a major effort to be directed by the LEAA including formal grants to states, demonstration projects, research and evaluation of programs, and other technical assistance. Moreover, the following priorities emerged:

1. removal of status offenders from detention and correctional facilities;
2. diversion of status offenders from the juvenile justice system;
3. reduction of serious crimes committed by juveniles; and
4. prevention of delinquency.[8]

It is my impression that substantial progress has been made on the first two goals — by administrative fiat — while the remaining two goals have gone essentially unresolved.

---

[5]Weis and Sederstrom (1981), p. 18.
[6]U.S. Department of Justice (1976), p. 1.
[7]*Ibid.*
[8]*Ibid.*, p. 11.

Status Offenders.   First, let us determine whether the diversion of status offenders has been useful. Diversion assumes that an alternative means of intervention is *possible* and *available* (i.e., funded).   In my experience there are virtually no viable alternatives available to lower and middle income families for such "diversion." Initially, some funding was provided through LEAA and eventually through state resources. However, there is currently no movement in this direction. Probation officers in juvenile justice settings are not, in the main, trained as behavior-changers. Indeed, they often resort to the same ineffective tactics as parents: lecturing, discussing, asking "Why?," blaming, and threatening. Unfortunately, the "cat is out of the bag." Status offenders know that minimal legal consequences will be forthcoming. Often, they laugh at parents, judges, and probation officers who threaten dire consequences. Simply stated, there are none. This entire exercise seems to follow a common script from status offender to status offender.   Parents threaten — teenager repeats offense — detention home intake worker threatens — teenager repeats offense — judge threatens — teenager repeats offense — family gives up — teenager goes on to "bigger and better things." The status offender teenager is playing Russian roulette with the social system, maintaining his/her freedom while "chancing" some consequences. Instead of one in six as in the real game, the status offender has a lower chance of painful consequence, perhaps one of 100 or one in 200. It is no small wonder that status offenders frequently move on to more severe criminal acts.   If we as a society do not support parental rights in families of status offenders, we essentially shoot ourselves in the foot.

If the "new" system (circa 1974) is not useful or effective, what can be done? Ideally, a credible treatment program with status offenders would continue to isolate such teenagers from those with criminal records.   It is no use teaching them to be more effective and devious. Moreover, a continuum of services could be made available, ranging from family treatment by trained probation officers to residential treatment programs. I would like to see a thread run through each treatment approach stressing consequences — a strength of applied social learning theory — since it is a lack of effective consequences that is often missing from the behavioral histories of status offenders. Additionally, I would see an individual offender move from one modality (probation officer as caregiver) to a more restrictive setting if treatment were not effective. Such settings might include a group home or a therapeutic camping program.

I do not view the removal of status offenders from the justice system as a positive step. If a teenager will not comply with parental wishes, who would believe that a mental health professional or probation officer would fare any better? The force of law is needed to support entry into each modality, backed up by short-term incarceration for noncompliance. I have worked with countless teenagers who ran from treatment programs and refused to cooperate with treatment plans until parents and juvenile authorities agreed to a short stay in the "d-home." A few days with no contact from parents and peers will often do wonders for attitude. Often, incarceration is the only effective consequence.

Who is to coordinate and fund these efforts? In my experience, not the government *at any level!* The federal government has already thrown enough money at the problem — and failed. State governments have likewise been ineffective. The State of Alabama, where I practice, is probably no better or worse than any other. There are a few scattered group homes across the State with no common treatment technique and a dearth of beds (usually less than ten). Local governments can ill afford involvement for a variety of reasons, financial resources not among the least. Also, zoning fights over these programs are notoriously rough, and few local politicians will risk the wrath of an angry electorate. This is a job for the private sector.

By "private sector," I refer to several nongovernmental resources: organized religion, mental health practitioners, volunteer organizations, business and industry, and insurance companies. A continuum of treatment options developed by the private sector for status offenders would include the following:

> 1. Comprehensive parent training programs based on applied social learning theory. Courses would be conducted by mental health professionals.

> 2. A system of group homes based upon the Achievement Place model in which children would spend five days or more weekly in a highly structured environment (again, using the techniques of applied social learning theory). These group homes would be located within close proximity of the family and short-term treatment (3 to 6 months) would be the objective, returning the child to supervision of the parents on a gradual basis.

> 3. A state-wide system of therapeutic camps such as Campeonada near Rome, Georgia, (again based upon applied social learning theory). These programs would allow for more in-depth treatment and would be long-term in nature.

> 4. Short-term incarceration (less than 30 days) in facilities adjacent to but separate from serious offenders. This modality could be used, if necessary, at each preceding place of treatment when needed.

Once a child has been adjudicated a status offender, it would be important to delineate in clear, unambiguous terms the criteria for successful program completion. Status offenders need to be told the actual consequences of undesirable behavior and judges must be prepared to follow through with these consequences if the offender errs again: *Clear rules and certain consequences are needed.*

Funding for treatment of status offenders could be provided by a variety of private sources. Parents with adequate funds could assist in payment of fees. Insurance companies might be motivated to develop policies for treatment of status offenders. For those unable to pay all or part of the fee, assistance from religious organizations would be solicited. A national effort in this vein would include a call by the President and other leaders for volunteerism. The Department of Justice's Office of Juvenile Justice and Delinquency Prevention (OJJDP) could provide guidelines for operation of these programs (most of which are already in existence). It is my strong belief that such an undertaking would return control to the parents, respect to the courts, and fiscal responsibility to the OJJDP.

Serious Offenders. As noted earlier, juvenile crime is on the rise at alarming rates (with an occasional plateau, here and there). The Juvenile Justice and Delinquency Prevention Act was aimed at decreasing serious crime by juvenile offenders. However, when the regulations and mandates trickled down to the states, not much was ever done in a positive sense. The overall thrust of the Act has been to dilute justice for the serious juvenile offender. The Department of Youth Services (DYS) in Alabama has as one of its goals the incarceration of "as few youths as possible." Although it is claimed by DYS that all youths committed will stay at least six months, this is often not the case and the offender knows it. A juvenile judge can sentence an offender to DYS, but — the nature of the offense notwithstanding — DYS determines the actual sentence and facilities. Of course, the judge has an option to certify the offender as an "adult" and try him/her in adult court. However, the adult court judge frequently sees the crime as "a first offense" and places the offender on probation or assigns a light sentence — and the offender knows it. Parents no longer can say with certainty, "If you engage in such-and-such behavior and are caught by the authorities, you will go to prison." Offenders laugh at their parents' various threats and pursue their personal game of Russian roulette with the odds greatly in their favor.

The serious juvenile offender (e.g., one convicted of murder, armed robbery, rape) may be a troubled youth but he/she is primarily a threat to law abiding citizens. Society is no longer willing to ignore their deviancy or allow it to continue without consequence. For the sake of argument, assume that incarceration does not "cure" criminal behavior. I would argue that it does not — but we have not found anything else that has proven any more effective. It does deter the offender while incarcerated, undoubtedly. Therefore, it would seem appropriate to throw rehabilitation out the window for these violent individuals and provide extended periods of incarceration for *all* serious offenders. Another technique to try would be "group parole" where each paroled convict would be assigned to a group of four to six paroled individuals. If one member breaks parole, the whole group suffers a consequence. This would be peer pressure at its best! Whether the problem with rehabilitation is with the techniques available or the social system itself not accepting the paroled convict back into civilized living, the fact remains that prisons do not rehabilitate, *and* offenders in prison commit fewer crimes on ordinary citizens.

Tougher sentences and increased actual time served would affect parents' rights by giving the admonitions of parents validity and constancy and by promising and delivering unambiguous consequences for deviant behavior. In this way, the rights of compliance and respect are reiterated. Laws without consequences make a mockery of the juvenile justice system and, in my opinion, result in a higher probability of anti-social behavior.

Preventing Delinquency. As noted earlier, the Juvenile Justice and Delinquency Prevention Act had as an objective the "prevention of delinquency." This is a lofty ideal that I am not certain is attainable now. Although OJJDP has funded several research projects on delinquency prevention (e.g., the National Center for the Assessment of Delinquent Behavior and Its Prevention in Seattle), the jury is still out. Indeed, the methodological problems involved in conducting such research are extremely complex in a free society and may obviate the possibility of *ever* conducting definitive primary prevention studies in this area. Certainly, it is my impression that the entire problem of juvenile crime and its prevention requires more thought and basic research than has heretofore been performed. Social scientists have consistently promised much and delivered less. Funding efforts by the federal government would best be directed at training social scientists in research methodology and at small, basic research programs. We simply do not know enough about the entire subject to risk large amounts of funds in full scale primary prevention projects in this area.

Family Planning

With the *Roe v. Wade*[9] decision, the Supreme Court opened the door to the rampant use of abortion as a birth control technique. In Alabama, a 14-year-old can legally obtain a therapeutic abortion *in complete confidence*. Parents are not notified or involved unless the mother-to-be so requests. Moreover, a physician can legally provide a 14-year-old with birth control pills or other devices in complete confidence. Parents of minor children are often routinely excluded from the decision-making process. This is a certain violation of parental rights (i.e., being informed and influencing children to behave in a manner inconsistent with parental beliefs) and has the result of weakening the family bond by diluting parental influence.

Accompanying the sexual revolution has been the teaching of sex education outside of the family. It was argued that families had abdicated their role as sex educators so state education boards, under national pressure, included sex education in the curriculum of public schools. Such education, it was agreed, would result in a lowered rate of unwanted pregnancies and venereal disease. What really happened was not predicted by these zealots. Sex education has been associated with increased sexual "experimentation" among teens and has not — by any measure — lowered the pregnancy rate in unmarried teenagers or the rate of venereal disease in the same population.

---

[9] 410 U.S. 113 (1973).

The most damaging blow, however, was directed at the family itself. Parents were excluded from making decisions with respect to their children's health and morality, a violation of one of their most important rights. Despite parents' *responsibility* for teenagers' behaviors, critical tools for influencing their behaviors were withdrawn. Other authorities were injected into the family such as physicians, social workers, teachers, and counselors. Parents were not privy to the most intimate behaviors of their children while outsiders helped shape and determine the destinies of children and the unborn. Predictably, advertisements of family planning services for teens stress the "confidential" nature of their services.

What should public policy be in this matter? Aside from the moral issue of abortion, parents of minor children should — by law — be required to approve any medical procedure or prescription administered. When parents are involved, their counsel would be given validity in other areas; when excluded, their influence in other areas wanes. In our culture, parents are held legally and morally responsible for their children's behavior. Excluding them from some aspects of decision-making, particularly in such an intimate area as sexual conduct, diminishes parents' ability to carry out their responsibilities effectively.

Sex education should be taught — but to *parents* of young children. Why not allow parents to develop their own curriculum in the home and have professional consultants available along with appropriate materials? Schools and churches could develop study modules from which parents could pick and choose. I do not believe that sex education by public educators is the logical option, in lieu of its absence in the home, particularly in light of the failure of such education to reach its stated objectives and its long-term negative effects on the family.

Legal Drinking Age

A final area of consideration is that of the legal drinking age and its effect on family life. Consider the following facts, presented recently at the 97th Congress of the National Institute on Alcohol Abuse and Alcoholism, Division of Prevention:

1. approximately 26,000 people are killed annually in America by drunk drivers;
2. one out of 10 drivers on a weekend night is legally intoxicated;
3. only one in every 2000 drunk drivers will ever be apprehended;
4. 44% of all fatal, nighttime alcohol-related crashes are caused by drivers 16 to 24 years old (22% of all licensed drivers fall in this bracket);
5. 75% of American youth consume alcohol by age 16; and
6. 59% of high school males have had drinking and driving difficulties; 42% of high school females have had drinking and driving difficulties.[10]

These data are astounding, and, yet, there are those who want to lower the drinking age even further. The legal age for purchase and consumption of alcoholic beverages in Alabama is 19. My impression is that lowered legal drinking age results in more teenagers being influenced by their older peers and at an earlier age. In my practice, I am seeing more and more alcoholic teens and pre-teens, partly a result of the peer pressure exerted and partly because of the lowered legal age for purchase. Without question, the most abused drug of adolescents is alcohol — and in *epidemic* proportions.

It is my contention that a lowered age for legalized use of alcoholic beverages is disruptive of family life and violates parental rights. First, many 19-year-old adolescents are still dependent on their parents and, therefore, ostensibly under their protection and care. The lowered drinking age takes the

---

[10]Statistics from the 97th Congress of the National Institute on Alcohol Abuse and Alcoholism, Division of Prevention.

responsibility of drinking out of the hands of parents and places the bottle in the hands of adolescents, who, as we have seen, have an unenviable record of misuse and abuse. Second, the availability of alcohol seems to "trickle down" with legal purchasers buying for younger teens below the legal age. Again, this needlessly interjects outsiders (from the family nucleus) into the family. Third, it often pits parents against other authorities who tell them it is alright to drink alcohol and "get a buzz." Admittedly, outside influences have always been around, but why aid and abet the enemy? There are those who argue that "if he's old enough to fight for his country, he's old enough to drink." On the contrary, one could argue that the data available support the notion that "he may be old enough to drink but he's not mature enough to handle it." Why not protect ourselves and our teens and *raise* the legal drinking age and the draft age to 27? A better saying would be: "If he's old enough to drink *responsibly*, he's old enough to fight for our country."

An issue related to legal drinking age is that of the legal consequences for drunk drivers. I am pleased to report that this cloud is developing a silver lining. Mothers Against Drunk Drivers (MADD) has mounted a far-reaching and effective battle in every state. Alabama's laws in this regard have been strengthened — the consequences of drunk driving are now more severe than ever. Unfortunately, that is not saying much but it is a step. If one believes that behavior is largely a function of its consequences (and *I* assume this), more severe consequences for drunk drivers should lower deaths due to intoxicated drivers. Coupled with a much higher legal age for drinking, we could conceivably cut the rate in half. Does one have a "civil right" to drink at age 19 or 21? Not at all. Ask the relatives of the 8000 teenagers and young adults who are killed each year in drinking and driving accidents whose civil rights have been violated.

Alcohol is so ingrained in our national fiber that its effects on the family often go unnoticed. Seventy-five percent of the adult convicts I have evaluated are heavy drinkers, and most were intoxicated during the commission of their crimes. Alcohol has a disinhibiting effect on behavior as it finds its way into the bloodstream. After it has been metabolized, it may effect the user's behavior for days or weeks. The aldehyde residue is often associated with lowered performance and diminished motivation, irritability, and easy distractibility. Academic studies are often neglected, defensiveness appears, and interests may become limited and constricted. These symptoms may be manifested when the user is sober, long after the metabolic process has eliminated the alcohol from the body. Parents are often not knowledgeable about the after-effects of heavy alcohol use and may be unaware that it is the cause of noncompliance, disrespect, illegal or immoral behavior, and secretiveness in their children. Again, the assumption of parental rights by the state is insidious and subtle — and, I believe, unintentional.

Treating alcohol abuse as a status offense seems reasonable and appropriate. A judge could offer a juvenile alcoholic the choice of treatment or spending time in detention (a lopsided choice, admittedly). More serious offenses such as driving under the influence of alcohol require more severe consequences. I would consider a *long* stay in detention (e.g., 45 days) an appropriate treatment and loss of drivers license for six months a baseline penalty for the first offense. If we really want to help parents control their children's deviancy and protect the rest of us, strong sanctions are warranted and necessary. Such severe consequences would enhance parental advice to abstain from alcohol and from mixing alcohol with driving.

If the courts are allowed to do what the public (and common sense) requires, parental rights are strengthened. Rules of social intercourse and conduct would be enforced by clear, unambiguous consequences. Parents would not be perceived as merely "blowing smoke." Their commands and rules would have the support of the entire social system.

Recommendations

As I have indicated, it is my contention that federal and state government action designed to alleviate problems of families and children is often ill conceived and iatrogenic. I have several recommendations on the general nature of legislation affecting parents and children.

First, we should make Congress and state legislative bodies tell us ahead of time what effects specific legislation is likely to have. Obviously, a general, philosophical discourse will not suffice. When a bill's author tells us that it will "prevent juvenile delinquency," this says little about the desired effects. It would be more useful to have one or more clear, unambiguous, and measurable statements as to purpose (e.g., "decrease the number of arrests of juveniles from the ages of 15 to 19 for murder and rape and aggravated assault by 25%" or "increase the percentage of convictions for these offenses from 15% to 60%"). Moreover, it would be useful to define time constraints (e.g., "such and such will happen by 1987"). In this manner, other legislators would not be buying a "pig in a poke"; the precise purpose of the legislation would be clear. Moreover, continued funding of projects could be made on the basis of merit (if not, it would be patently obvious). Did it do what the author(s) hoped?

In order to initiate this approach, the government could develop a pool of private consultants to assist in developing evaluation criteria (nothing elaborate, just tools for measurement). These consultants would coordinate modest evaluation procedures and subsequently present their data for legislative perusal. This may make the system difficult enough to discourage the passage of some bills. At least, we as consumers of government services and taxpayers would be capable of making educated judgments regarding the efficacy of governmental interventions. If we are to be an "experimenting society" (as my liberal friends often expound), let us be scientific.

Second, an enhanced sensitivity to parental rights is needed in legislative circles. In the heat of the moment, viewing juvenile delinquents' behaviors as symptomatic of immaturity, poor parenting, or as a function of social ills may have disastrous consequences. Blaming the parents does not solve the problem, *it merely accentuates it by lowering parental motivation and control.* Again, legislation with the purported aim of enhancing children's rights should be subject to great skepticism and scrutiny.

Third, as I suggested earlier, the involvement of the private sector in the development of resources for families with problems would be of inestimable value. This is not a trite, off-the-cuff recommendation. The private sector commitment to programs it develops and supports is stronger and more persistent. When government enters into these social efforts, the humaneness of the helping relationship is lost. Recipients begin to assume the *right* of such services and become less "reinforcing" to the caregivers. Soon, caregivers lose their motivation in the absence of rewards like genuine thankfulness, and the system of "caregiving" changes to one of "service rendering," which is impersonal and ultimately ineffective. When families perceive that care is given out of concern and not bureaucratic necessity, interventions are more effective. Government, by its very nature, can never succeed in this endeavor because the legislative targets learn to expect certain services as a right of citizenship.

Fourth, the massive expenditures of financial resources at the federal level aimed at family matters is of highly questionable value. It would seem difficult for even the most dogmatic liberal to assert that a dispassionate, remote individual in Washington cares as much for our children as we do. There is no evidence of which I am aware to justify the continued funding of demonstration grants in child abuse, juvenile justice, and other attempts at caregiving. Demonstration grants are notorious as being bottomless pits with minimal dissemination. Why do we as a society persist in this waste of taxpayers' money? The reason is simply stated: "pork barrel" politics.

Fifth, our children are bombarded between five and seven hours daily by the Video Monster which provides a variety of misinformation and teaches maladaptive behaviors. Violence and sex on TV have reached epidemic proportions. Research now suggests a clear correlation between violent acts on TV and aggressive acts by children. The virtues of alcohol and drug use are touted nightly. Premarital sex is the norm. Everyone is a manager, and most businessmen are crooked. Religion is a figment of one's imagination and not important. Christians are "uncool." Problems can be solved quickly and with great certainty. Liberals love people and are the "good guys"; conservatives love big business and war and are the "bad guys."

I am opposed to government censorship of television. Consumers of TV must be the ones to put it in order. If they refused to watch sleazy shows, their ratings would fall and the shows would be dropped. Better yet, a boycott of products advertised during the inappropriate programs would create a voice more thunderous than a tornado. In this way, the market place would truly call the shots.

Sixth, an overall emphasis on the family as the locus of change efforts is required. We must stop the dangerous trend of looking to Big Brother and Uncle Sam for help. Relying on the resources of the family and giving aid and comfort to parents would represent a step in the right direction. Strengthening parental skill and shoring up parental influence will result in a new vitality and confidence in family living, which is the backbone of our way of life. Would you rather have Uncle Sam or Mom and Dad caring for our children? The choice is yours.

State Intervention in the Family and Parental Rights: A Legal Assessment

Robert J. D'Agostino

Social development theory confirms the central role of the family in the development of the child. Dr. Rinn has reviewed this in his paper. Without a firm foundation provided by the parents, a child's prognosis for successful adjustment is not good. A successful family experience correlates with success in school, with the ability to resist peer pressure, and with later economic and social achievement.[1]

The home and family as an institution has grown out of the very nature of man. It has come out of the needs of men and women for each other, for cooperation in life and work, and out of the necessity of the loving care children require for emotional security and maturity. At one time, without the benefit of modern social development research, courts knew the central role of the family. This is seen in the following quotes:

> Marriage . . . creat[es] the most important relation in life . . . [and] ha[s] more to do with the morals and civilization of a people than any other institution. . . .[2]

---

[1]See Roger Rinn's paper in this book.
[2]*Maynard v. Hill*, 125 U.S. 190, 205 (1888).

The law views marriage as . . . a civil contract . . . except that
it is not revocable or dissoluble at the will of the parties.[3]

The exercise of parental authority is not necessarily for the
profit of the parent, but for the advantage of the child. . . .
[The parent's] right to personal custody and personal
service are secured to him, therefore, in order that through
them, prompted by natural affection, he may successfully
impart to them habits of industry, methods of thrift and the
means of personal success in life.[4]

Being a parent imposes both a legal and moral duty.[5] Those
duties were said to include the duties of maintenance,[6]
protection,[7] and education.[8] The family as an institution was
seen to have economic, protective, religious, recreational, and
educational functions:

Two outstanding conclusions are indicated by the data
on changes in family life. One is the decline of the
institutional functions of the family, as for example its
economic functions. Thus the family now produces less
food and clothing than it did formerly. The teaching
functions of the family also have been largely shifted to
another institution, the school. Industry and the state have
both grown at the family's expense. The significance of this
diminution in the activities of the family as a group is far
reaching.

The other outstanding conclusion is the resulting
predominant importance of the personality functions of the
family — that is, those which provide for the mutual
adjustments among husbands, wives, parents and children
and for the adaptation of each member of the family to the
outside world. The family has always been responsible to a
large degree for the formation of character. It has furnished

---

[3]*In re Hulett's Estate*, 69 N.W. 31,33 (MN 1896).
[4]*Beaver, Bare & Co. v. Bare*, 104 Pa. 58, 62 (1883).
[5]*Gulley v. Gulley*, 231 S.W. 97, 98 (TX 1921).
[6]1 Blackstone's *Commentaries* 447.
[7]*Ibid.*, at 450; *State v. Douglass*, 101 S.W. 648 (SC 1919).
[8]*Cory v. Cook*, 24 R.I. 421 (1902).

> social contacts and group life. With the decline of its institutional functions these personality functions have come to be its most important contribution to society. The chief concern over the family nowadays is not how strong it may be as an economic organization but how well it performs services for the personalities of its members.[9]

The family may no longer be the institution which carries out these functions, however, as the following fact suggests:

> If we define the nuclear family as a working husband, a housekeeping wife, and two children, and ask how many Americans actually still live in this type of family, the answer is astonishing: 7%....[10]

What then should justify substituting the state's judgment for that of the parents with regard to the care and guidance of a particular child? What rationale does the state use to so substitute its judgment? The answer to the first question may be seen as fact-dependent; the second as reflecting the philosophical or ideological orientation of those making the decisions about which facts justify intervention.

The Factual Rationale for Intervention

Generally

The current explicit rationale for intervention by the state in the family is family violence. Legislative efforts generally focus on abused children and more recently, battered wives, the most common victims of family violence.

---

[9]Ogburn, William F., "The Family and its Functions" in Association of American Law Schools, *Selected Essays on Family Law* (Brooklyn, NY: Foundation Press, 1950), p. 20.

[10]Toffler, Alvin, *The Third Wave* (New York: Bantam Books, 1981), p. 211-212.

A distinction should and is generally made between what constitutes probable cause for the state's inquiring into a family relationship, particularly the parent-child relationship, and what is sufficient cause to terminate or modify that relationship. A further distinction is based on the status of being an adult (battered wife or elderly parents) and being a child (the state being more willing to intervene against the expressed wishes of child and parent alike).

In 1974, the Federal Child Abuse Prevention and Treatment Act,[11] creating the National Center on Child Abuse and Neglect, mandated federal research into the causes and prevention of child abuse and provided for the publication of information and training materials. Grants were made to states whose progress met ten specified requirements which are largely procedural.[12]

Generally, state laws provide for the independent representation of children who are the subject of child protection proceedings. The role of the representative is often stated to be to serve the best interests of his client — the child.

Abused and Neglected Children

The protection of abused children started out as a private effort with state governments only recently assuming a major role.[13] By the 1970's, state legislation defined abuse and neglect, created agencies to investigate claims of abuse and to provide protective services, and mandated that certain professionals who deal with the child report suspected abuse and neglect cases.[14]

---

[11]42 U.S.C. Secs. 5101-5106 (1976; and Supp. III, 1980).

[12]Schechter, Lowell F., "The Violent Family and the Ambivalent State: Developing a Coherent Policy for State Aid to Victims of Family Violence," 20 *Journal of Family Law* 1 at pp. 4-7 (1981-1982).

[13]*Ibid.*, p. 2.

[14]Paulsen, M.G., "The Law and Abused Children," in *The Battered Child*, Helfer, Ray E. and Kempe, C. Henry, eds. (Chicago: U. of Chicago Press, 1974), pp. 175-200.

Douglas J. Besharov summarizes the initial responsibilities of a child protective agency as:

> (1) providing immediate protection to children, through temporary stabilization of the home environment or, where necessary, protective custody;
> (2) verifying the validity of the report and determining the danger to the children;
> (3) assessing the service needs of children and families;
> (4) providing or arranging for protective, ameliorative, and treatment services; and
> (5) instituting civil court action when necessary, to remove a child from a dangerous environment or to impose treatment on his family.[15]

Although much legislation did not originally clearly differentiate between status offenders, delinquents, and abused and neglected children, often lumping the first two together or classifying some abused and neglected children as status offenders, that situation is rapidly changing.[16]

Many states have enacted all or part of the Uniform Juvenile Court Act and follow the Model Rules for Juvenile Courts. The modern trend is to merge the once independent juvenile courts into a more inclusive family court, with the theory being that children's problems ordinarily cannot be separated or dealt with effectively without jurisdiction over the parents. This would certainly be a good idea if the courts assisted and *worked through* the parents.

Starting with *In re Gault*,[17] several procedural safeguards, including the right to counsel, have spread from juvenile delinquency to other types of hearings involving adversarial interests. Statutes vary from providing for an absolute right to

---

[15]Besharov, Douglas J., "The Legal Aspects of Reporting Known and Suspected Child Abuse and Neglect," 23 *Villanova Law Rev.* 458, 495 (1978).

[16]See Roger Rinn's paper.

[17]387 U.S. 1 (1967).

counsel for the abused or neglected child, to allowing discretion by the judge, to providing for no right to counsel or the appointment of a non-lawyer guardian *ad litem*.

Unlike delinquency cases, in abuse and neglect cases, and perhaps in some status offender cases, the court is dealing with the action of a child's parent or guardian. The court must weigh parental rights in the context of legislative and judicial law-making as to what circumstances justify intervention on behalf of a child.

Decisions in individual cases are generally made with reference to a statute or a court decision. Hence, when we talk of state intervention, we are primarily referring to the legislative and judicial branches and the effect statutes and judicial decisions have on the way the administrative or executive agencies function or look at an issue.

Although the rhetoric of the state's commitment to family privacy and parental autonomy has remained the same, it is apparent that the scope and meaning of those terms has changed dramatically. The legislature's intrusions have historically consisted of setting relatively precise limits on parental judgment concerning matters about which there is a clear societal consensus.[18] Compulsory education laws, limitations on child labor, and immunization requirements are all infringements on parental autonomy. The very act of intervention as a result of an abuse or neglect proceeding is in itself an intrusion that will probably change the family relationship forever.[19]

The definitions of what constitutes abuse and neglect are undergoing change, and the expansion of these definitions bode ill for family integrity.

---

[18]See generally, Goldstein, Joseph; Freud, Anna; and Solnit, Albert J., *Before the Best Interests of the Child* (New York: Free Press, 1979).
[19]*Ibid.*

What is "Neglect"?

The Illinois Supreme Court defined "neglect" as follows:

> Neglect . . . is the failure to exercise the care that the circumstances justly demand. It embraces willful as well as unintentional disregard of duty. It is not a term of fixed and measured meaning. It takes its context always from specific circumstances, and its meaning varies as the context of surrounding circumstances changes.[20]

Such an expansive definition, standing alone, seems open-ended, bounded only by the discretion of the intervening state agency. Equally boundless is this excerpt from the Report of the President's Commission on Law Enforcement and Administration of Justice made in 1967, to wit, "The neglect jurisdiction of the juvenile court should be retained since it involves conflicts between the parents' right to custody and the child's physical and *mental* well being."[21]

Contrast these definitions with the outlook of some early cases which held that "where the father neglects his duty to furnish support and necessaries to his infant children, and their wants are supplied by others, the law will imply a promise on his part to pay for such necessaries. . . . It seems that the father should be held liable only where the service rendered or supplies furnished were absolutely necessary to relieve the child from actual want."[22] This "rule" of neglect was certainly clear but no longer states the parameters of what is neglect. The newer rules stated previously are not much more helpful. However, most

---

[20]*People ex rel. Wallace v. Labrenz*, 104 N.E. 2d 769, 773 (IL 1952).

[21]*The Challenge of Crime in a Free Society*, Report of the President's Commission on Law Enforcement and Administration of Justice (Washington, DC: U.S. Government Printing Office, 1967), p. 85, emphasis added.

[22]Long, Joseph R., *A Treatise on the Law of Domestic Relations*, 3rd ed. (Indianapolis: Bobbs-Merrill Co., 1923), p. 435 and footnotes cited therein.

courts have been rather unwilling to be as open ended as the neglect definitions invite them to be.

Although "the best interest of the child" is the standard used to determine custody in divorce and separation proceedings,[23] that test is not generally accepted in parental termination proceedings[24] and may or may not be the standard applied in parental rights modification proceedings.[25]

The Oregon Court of Appeals held that before the best interests of a child may be considered in a parental termination case, there must be evidence of willful abandonment or neglect of the child. Mere failure to support or see the child is not enough when the parent knows the child is well cared for and has sufficient cause not to see him (agreement with the mother in this case).[26]

Courts generally state that the burden of proving the custodial unfitness of the parent rests on the party seeking to deprive the parent of custody.[27] It may be seen that by reasoning thus, the court builds in a bias in favor of parents. In fact, the common law rule was in favor of the father except in the case of an illegitimate child where the mother enjoyed a *prima facie* right to custody. Later, the "tender years" doctrine established a presumption in favor of mothers generally. In either case, the natural right of parents doctrine prevailed, finding expression in the Supreme Court opinion in *Meyer v. Nebraska*[28] which held that the right to "marry, establish a home and bring up children" are among "those privileges long recognized at common law as

---

[23]See generally, Kram, Shirley Wohl and Frank, Neil A., *The Law of Child Custody: Development of the Substantive Law* (Lexington, MA: Lexington Books, 1982).

[24]*Ibid.*

[25]*Ibid.*

[26]*Mahoney v. Linder*, 514 P. 2d 901 (Ore. 1973); cf *Dunne v. McCashum*, 508 P. 2d 821 (OR 1973).

[27]*Kropp v. Shepsky*, 113 N.E. 2d 801 (NY 1953).

[28]262 U.S. 390 (1923).

essential to the orderly pursuit of happiness by free men."[29] Following that decision, a New York case held that "the right of a parent, under natural law, to establish a home and bring up children is a fundamental one and beyond the reach of any court."[30]

The rise of the child's rights movement threatens this pro-family bias. Rather than any deference given to the parents per se and to their views on the proper upbringing of a child, the child rights advocates believe that when the parents "threaten the autonomous growth and expression" of a child, there is no reason to protect family autonomy. This attitude finds expression in Iowa where the "best interests of the child" test predominates. Although advocates would undoubtedly disapprove of the decision by the Iowa court in a case some years ago, they can't fault the reasoning. The court awarded custody of a child to the maternal grandparents rather than the natural father who was acknowledged to be unfit because the court, that is the judge, decided he liked the grandparents' lifestyle better than the father's.[31] The import is that whatever one thinks of the lifestyles involved, the judge ruled on his preferences and not on the fitness issue. The preference was for a locally culturally conforming lifestyle. This is not an isolated case, being reaffirmed in Iowa in a subsequent case which cited with approval the section of the Model Custody Act adopted by the Family Law Section of the American Bar Association in 1963. That provided that "[c]ustody may be awarded to persons other than the father or mother whenever such award serves the best interests of the child. Any person who has *de facto* custody of the child in a stable and wholesome home and is a fit and proper person shall *prima facie* be entitled to an award of custody." Before pulling back somewhat from the "best interests"

---

[29]*Ibid.* at 399.

[30]*Portnoy v. Strasser*, 104 N.E. 2d 895, 896 (NY 1952).

[31]*Painter v. Bannister*, 140 N.W. 2d 152 (Iowa 1966), *cert. denied*, 384 U.S. 949 (1966).

doctrine,[32] Iowa courts explicitly rejected the natural rights of parents doctrine in stating "it has been said that the 'natural right' concept restricts thoughtful inquiry into latent problems of child development and should not be permitted to control. . . ."[33] This explicitly opens the courts to behavioral and sociological fads as a basis for decisions on this matter.

From negligence, meaning "failure to provide necessaries," to gross failures of parental care such as leaving young children unsupervised in potentially dangerous situations, to finding neglect on the basis of "the best interests of the child," is an odyssey that leads from focusing on the actions of a parent to the presumed needs of a child as determined in an adversarial proceeding with expert witnesses and the state (a judge) as decision-maker. With the strong presumption in favor of the natural rights of parents, state agency discretion was effectively limited. Without such a presumption, discretion is limited only by the inclinations of the decision-makers.

What is "Abuse"?

Courts have said the following about child abuse:

> It must be shown that the parents *subjected*, or allowed another to subject, the child to mistreatment or abuse. . . . Further, it must be shown that the condition resulting from the alleged abuse is not *justifiably explained* . . . [the state] must prove these elements by a preponderance of the evidence.[34]

> In Child Protective proceedings it is the function of the trial court to determine not only that neglect or abuse exist, but also whether it is *likely* to exist.[35] [Here the parents had

---

[32]See *Matter of Burney*, 259 N.W. 2d 322 (Iowa 1977).

[33]*Garvin v. Garvin*, 152 N.W. 2d 206, 211 (Iowa 1967).

[34]*In re People in the Interest of R.K. and S.K.*, 505 P. 2d 37, 38 (CO 1972). Emphasis is the opinion's.

[35]*In the Matter of Baby Boy Santos*, 336 N.Y.S. 2d 817, 820 (Fam. Ct. N.Y.C. 1972). Emphasis is the opinion's.

abused another of their children and the court was concerned with the child abuse syndrome.]

Failure to provide emergency or life-saving medical treatment is variously labeled abuse or neglect which does not warrant termination or modification of parental custody except for the purpose of the treatment ordered.

Unfit Parents

In determining whether parents are unfit, courts have historically looked to the specific grounds set forth in the statute. The "best interests" test has not generally been used, at least in the absence of abandonment or neglect. Typical is the following: "Since there must be strict and literal compliance with the statutory requirements . . . we cannot consider the best interests of the child as sufficient justification to terminate . . . parental rights."[36] Continued abuse, willful abandonment, and an inability to care for the child in the future are all grounds relied on to terminate parental rights. A more recent development is the consideration of "psychological fitness,"[37] generally in the context of a custody battle between parents. Courts talk about "warmth" versus being "regimented," and "positive input into the child's development."[38]

Recent cases alleging that custodial third parties are the "psychological parents" and hence the rights of the natural parents should be terminated have generally been decided on whether the natural parents have actually abandoned the children.[39] However, psychological parent arguments often are made using the "best interests of the child" standard in

---

[36]*In re M.J.M.*, 483 S.W. 2d 795, 798 (MO 1972).

[37]See *Mouscardy v. Mouscardy*, 405 N.Y.S. 2d 759 (2d Dept. 1978).

[38]See, for example, *Montagna v. Krok*, 404 N.Y.S. 2d 41, 42 (2d Dept. 1978); *Salk v. Salk*, 393 N.Y.S. 2d 841 (Sup. Ct. 1975) *aff'd* 385 N.Y.S. 2d 1015 (1st Dept. 1976) cited and discussed in Kram and Frank, note 24, p. 53.

[39]See *Montagna v. Krok, supra.*

derogation of the natural rights of the parents standard. Even states like New York, which nominally follow the natural right theories, have weakened that standard by applying an "extraordinary circumstances" test to terminate natural parental rights in the absence of unfitness or abandonment.[40]

In general, we should not expect the state to provide solutions. Richard J. Gelles writes that state intervention in response to child abuse typically fails and holds little hope for solving the problem.[41]

The Philosophical Rationale for Intervention

Generally

The Ninth Amendment to the Constitution provides that, "The enumeration in the Constitution, of certain rights, shall not be construed to deny or disparage others retained by the people."

The amendment makes no sense unless it is understood that the drafters meant the Bill of Rights as a protection of rights already granted by the natural law or clearly recognized by the common law.[42] This amendment made it clear that the enumeration of rights to be protected against federal power (presumably also against state power now via the Fourteenth Amendment), did not imply that the other natural or fundamental rights[43] not mentioned were abandoned.

Assuming there *is* a right to privacy, why have the courts recently restricted that to individuals? In fact, they have used that right to "protect" the individual child against the parents to, in effect, leave the child to the "tender loving care" of the state.

---

[40]See *Bennett v. Jeffreys*, 387 N.Y.S. 2d 821 (1976).

[41]Gelles, Richard J., *Family Violence*, Vol. 84, Sage Library of Social Research (Beverly Hills, CA: Sage, 1979), p. 40 and Part I generally.

[42]See Raphael T. Waters' paper in this book.

[43]See *Davis v. Firment*, 269 F. Supp. 524 (D.C. La. 1967), *aff'd* 408 F. 2d 1085 (5th Cir. 1967).

How can the state love a child? How can the state deal with the problem of the unloved child?

One group of experts writes the following:

> As *parens patriae* the state is too crude an instrument to become an adequate substitute for flesh and blood parents. The legal system has neither the resources nor the sensitivity to respond to a growing child's ever changing needs and demands. It does not have the capacity to deal on an individual basis with the consequences of its decision. . . .[44]

On the one hand, the state claims *parens patriae* privileges to terminate and modify parents' rights in the interests of a child, while, on the other hand, the state purposely undermines parental moral control of the child. In New York, a court dismissed a delinquency case against a girl who had engaged in prostitution, saying the conduct was not illegal if done by an adult, therefore, it would not be the basis of a proceeding against a minor — it was, after all, harmless commercial sex. The state is increasingly not assisting parents in the "status offender" cases, relying on the fiction that children are just like adults, hence, standards applicable to adults are applicable to children.

The resulting judicialization of the parent/child relationship is what is behind the privacy decisions in the abortion areas and in the changing view of marriage implicit in "life" decisions generally. In *Planned Parenthood v. Danforth,*[45] Missouri contended that marriage is an institution, the nature of which places limitations on absolute individualism. Clearly, the abortion decisions view the marriage relationship as contractual — two separate individuals with no merger.[46] Missouri argued that marriage is covenantal (i.e., decisions must be mutual). The court said it cannot delegate to a spouse that which it is powerless to do, i.e., the right to abortion is a personal right of

---

[44]Goldstein *et al*, p. 12.

[45]428 U.S. 52 (1976).

[46]Compare, the law of tenants by the entireties.

the mother, the father has no right except the procreational right of making the wife pregnant with her consent.

It is a small step from saying that marriage is merely contractual to saying the parent/child relationship is merely contractual. That is exactly what the child rights advocates are really saying, and that is exactly what the logical extension of the "best interests" test means. Child rights advocates make no bones about "re-allocating" parenthood. Age becomes a suspect classification. *Bellotti v. Baird*,[47] on the minor's right to abortion, is a direct threat to family ties encouraging deception, silence, and guilt. One legal commentator has written the following about this:

> The federal judiciary's refusal to countenance any parental *participation* or consultation in the minor's abortion decision-making is in reality an attempt to avoid or settle an intra-family doctrinal dispute over matters of health, religion, or morality by "protecting" the minor from her own parents.[48]

Changing Views of the Supreme Court

The following is the language once used by the Supreme Court:

> [L]iberty . . . denotes not merely bodily restraint but also the right of the individual . . . to marry, establish a home and bring up children . . . and generally to enjoy those privileges long recognized at common law as essential to the orderly pursuit of happiness by free men.[49]

---

[47]428 U.S. 132 (1976). See also *Planned Parenthood v. Danforth*, 428 U.S. 52 (1976).

[48]Riga, Peter J., "Decision-Making Within the Family: Who Decides?," 23 *South Tex. L.J.* 95, 123. Emphasis is Riga's.

[49]*Meyer v. Nebraska*, 262 U.S. 390, 399 (1923).

The child is not the mere creature of the State; those who nurture him and direct his destiny have the right, coupled with the high duty, to recognize and prepare him for additional obligations.[50]

It is cardinal with us that the custody, care and nurture of the child reside first in the parents, whose primary function and freedom include preparation for obligations the state can neither supply nor hinder. . . . And it is in recognition of this that . . . decisions have respected the private realm of family life which the state cannot enter. . . . But the family itself is not beyond regulation in the public interest . . . [the] rights of parenthood are [not] beyond limitation. . . . The state's authority over children's activities is broader than over like actions of adults.[51]

. . . it seems clear that if the state is empowered, as *parens patriae*, to "save" a child from himself or his Amish parents by requiring an additional two years of . . . education [the case involved the right of Amish parents to refuse to send their children to secondary school], the State will in large measure influence, if not determine, the religious future of the child.[52]

Compare the foregoing to the following in another Supreme Court opinion:

It is the future of the student, not the future of the parents, that is imperiled in today's decision [*Yoder*]. . . . It is the student's judgment, not his parents', that is essential if we are to give full meaning to what we have said about the Bill of Rights and the right of students to be masters of their own destiny. If he is harnessed to the Amish way of life . . . his entire life may be stunted and deformed.[53]

---

[50]*Pierce v. Society of Sisters*, 268 U.S. 510, 535 (1925).
[51]*Prince v. Massachusetts*, 321 U.S. 158, 166, 168 (1944).
[52]*Wisconsin v. Yoder*, 406 U.S. 205, 232 (1972).
[53]Dissent of Justice Douglas in *Wisconsin v. Yoder* at 245-246.

Further, decisions based on the right to privacy have found that that right protects the right of unmarried adults to seek "sexual gratification."[54] Increasingly, the Supreme Court sees the right to privacy as an individual right independent of any relationship.

The Current Legal Climate

It is increasingly apparent that as natural law doctrines have been replaced by positivist legal theories, the concept of the family as a unit, created as independent and prior to the state, is waning. Marriage is now frequently viewed as just another contract, its covenantal nature forgotten or ignored; children are frequently seen as primarily wards of the state, with parents having only such rights as the law-makers might grant. The extreme view holds that childrearing is a function to be delegated to parents by the governing authority (usually a judge) on the basis of an abstract "best interests of the child" test.

Although the focus of this book is parental rights, the questions arising pertinent to this analysis are much broader. First, who retains rights and who enforces these retained rights? Second, how do we know which rights are retained? Are these rights changing? If so, what is the mechanism for their change? These were questions some have tried to answer. Perhaps the past can guide us to a more satisfying and effective current accommodation.

In discussing the rights of the American people in the debate over the Amnesty Bill in 1872, Senator Sherman said the following:

> . . . these amendments to the Constitution [i.e., the Bill of Rights] do not define all the rights of American citizens. They define some of them. The Constitution itself amply

---

[54]*People v. Onofre*, 51 N.Y.S. 2d 476, 488, 415 N.E. 2d 936, 940 (1980), *cert. denied*, 451 U.S. 987 (1981).

secures some of the rights of American citizens, but the ninth amendment expressly provides that, "The enumeration in the Constitution of certain rights shall not be construed to deny or disparage others retained by the people".... Where do we find the record of those rights? ... The great fountainhead, the great reservoir of the rights of an American citizen is in the common law.... Our rights are not limited to those given by the Constitution. What are those rights? ... You must go to the common law for them....[55]

Family rights are among the rights which antedate and underlie the Constitution.[56]

The child's rights advocates, at least implicitly, hold that the state is prior to the family, hence, all its rights flow from the state. These kinds of rights are at the expense of someone else's rights — ultimately based upon current policy preferences. These state absolutists are joined by those with an atomistic view of individuals. Both end up being *democratic totalitarians*; all individuals end up naked before the state. Peter L. Berger and Richard John Neuhaus write the following:

Without institutionally reliable processes of mediation, the political order becomes detached from the values and realities of individual life. Deprived of its moral foundation, the political order must be secured by coercion rather than by consent. And when that happens, democracy disappears....

The attractiveness of totalitarianism ... is that it overcomes the dichotomy of private and public existence by imposing on life one comprehensive order of meaning.[57]

---

[55]*The Congressional Globe* (Washington, DC: Congressional Globe Office, 1872), p. 843.

[56]*Amstead v. U.S.*, 277 U.S. 428 (1928).

[57]Berger, Peter L. and Neuhaus, Richard John, *To Empower People: The Role of Mediating Structures in Public Policy* (Washington, DC: American Enterprise Inst., 1977), p. 3.

Conclusion

The legal assault on the family conducted, of course, in the jargon of "rights" cannot be separated from the social disintegration which has occurred. Virtue is not taught, sexual promiscuity is not condemned in moral terms, the state condones and encourages deviousness and secretiveness in children's relationship with parents and then funds research into the causes and cures of delinquency.

The two most important mediating structures, religion and the family, are under attack. It is no coincidence that modern totalitarian regimes (whether fascist, National Socialist, or Communist-socialist) fight and suppress religion and, as a matter of policy, turn children against parents. Nazi Germany, as well as Communist Cuba, recruited children as informers. What better way to destroy family intimacy?

Both the extreme libertarians and the philosophical positivists who dominate legal education see right as only possessed by individuals. The status of marriage or parenthood is not seen as conferring special or different rights. In addition, positivists see all rights as emanating from the state. Obligations are seen only as contractual. Legislators are confused and the courts waffle. If the American people understand what is at stake, common sense will prevail, because the common law in its highest form is based on the nature of man, the *natural law* so eloquently discussed by Dr. Waters in his paper.

Child Abuse:
Pseudo-Crisis, Dangerous
Bureaucrats, Destroyed Families

Stephen M. Krason

Whenever we speak about parental rights today, it is necessary to consider the issue of child abuse/neglect. (Hereinafter, in referring to the problem generally, I shall simply speak of "child abuse." It should be understood that I mean both abuse and neglect when using the term.) There is now much public attention focused on it, and, when perpetrated or allegedly perpetrated by parents, the state intervenes and usually in some way interferes with, disrupts, alters, or terminates the rights of parents, temporarily or permanently, to control or carry on their relationship with their children. We have seen in Dr. Waters's paper how parental rights — along with parental obligations — are *natural*, so whenever we speak about interfering, restricting, or ending them, it is a very serious matter indeed, and one that should be approached with much prudence. Both the importance of natural rights *per se* and the centrality of the family for any society, as shown by Dr. Waters, mean that parental rights should not be infringed upon for "light and transient reasons." This essay will examine exactly how serious the child abuse problem is, how much child abuse is perpetrated by natural parents, how American laws are set up and implemented to deal with the problem and where they are flawed, and will give some perspectives both about why we have a child abuse problem, why the current response to it unjustly infringes on parental rights, and what should be done about it.

The Current State of the Child Abuse Problem

From the way child abuse is portrayed by the media, we get the impression it is of crisis proportions. But is it? Growing evidence says it is not. In fact, most reports of its occurrence are without foundation, and much of what is called "abuse" is not abuse at all. For the past ten years or so, a situation has existed in which a substantial majority of child abuse complaints have proved false. Writing about a study done in the late 1970s, Douglas J. Besharov, former Director of the National Center on Child Abuse and Neglect and a critic of overreporting tendencies of the current child abuse machinery, states that *65 percent* of child abuse reports in 1978 — involving a staggering 750,000 children — were "unfounded." Another study done in 1982 showed that half the parents whose families were placed under social service agency home supervision — somewhere between 400,000 and 500,000 families — "never actually maltreated their children." New York State, between 1979 and 1983, is a case in point. During this period, Besharov tells us that the number of child abuse reports increased by about 50 percent while substantiated cases declined by 20 percent. In round numbers, this means that while 20,000 additional families were investigated, the number of substantiated cases actually fell by 100.[1]

---

[1]Besharov, Douglas J., "'Doing Something' About Child Abuse: The Need to Narrow the Grounds for State Intervention," *Harvard Journal of Law and Public Policy*, Vol. 8, No. 3 (Summer 1985), pp. 556, 558, 566. His source for the 65 percent figure is: U.S. National Center on Child Abuse and Neglect, *National Analysis of Child Neglect and Abuse Reporting* (1978), p. 36, Table 28. His source for the 1982 study was

Besharov's earlier statistics about unfounded reports, then, continued to be borne out into the 1980s. In an article in the national lawyer's magazine *Case and Comment*, St. Petersburg, Florida attorney William D. Slicker cites more recent studies and sources: testimony before state hearings in Minnesota showed that over two-thirds of child abuse complaints could not be substantiated; the *Wall Street Journal* reported in 1985 that over 60 percent of child abuse reports are without validity; another study reported in the *Kansas City Times* in 1985 showed that 80 percent of child sex abuse cases are unfounded (double the figure of five years before); yet another study in *Marriage and Divorce Today* in 1985 established that in divorce-custody proceedings, where child abuse is frequently alleged nowadays, 70 percent of sex abuse charges have no basis.[2] All the while, we have seen a steady, precipitant increase in the number of child abuse reports, from 150,000 children affected in 1963 to 610,000 in 1972 — around the time the new, comprehensive child abuse reporting laws, discussed below, were starting to be put into effect — to 1.3 million in 1982. In 1984, over 1,024,000 *families* were reported, some of these reports involving more than one child.[3]

---

also the National Center. His source for the New York State figures is an official in the State Department of Social Services.

[2]Slicker, William D., "Child Sex Abuse: The Innocent Accused," *Case and Comment*, Vol. 91, No. 6 (Nov.-Dec. 1986), p. 14. He gives the citations to these other sources on this page: the Minnesota testimony was from the Berean League Task Force Interim Report, "Abuse of Parents' Rights and Child Abuse Laws"; *The Wall Street Journal* article appeared on October 10, 1985 and reported on a paper given by Drs. Diane Schetky and Harold Boverman at the Annual Meeting of the American Academy of Psychiatry and the Law in Albuquerque, N.M.; *The Kansas City Times* article was by Scott Kraft and appeared on February 11, 1985; the study about child abuse and custody proceedings appeared in *Marriage and Divorce Today*, Vol. 11, (Aug. 12, 1985).

[3]Besharov, p. 545 (see page for his sources); the 1984 statistics are from American Humane Association Highlights of Official Child

As far as even these figures about substantiated child abuse go — i.e., the reports that *have* some foundation — we cannot be sure that they are not inflated. This is because, as noted below, what is often included in them are entirely innocent acts that a social worker or other agent of the state chooses to define as "abuse," and that "substantiation" of a charge, especially of sexual abuse, may mean merely that a social worker is *suspicious* of a parent, even if there is no proof.[4]

How much child abuse is there, then? As we can see, not many more than a third of the staggering number of reports above really involve abuse. Mary Pride, in her book, *The Child Abuse Industry* — the best available compilation of information in one volume on the true nature of the child abuse problem and its threat to parental rights — discusses how grossly inaccurate normal media discussion of the amount of actual abuse is. Statistics given are "*estimates*, which means they are somebody's *guess*." They state such things as "'one out of every four children will be sexually abused by the time they are 18 . . . [and] [o]nly one out of every ten cases is reported.'" When you do a little calculating, she points out, this means that over 200 percent of the female population become sex abuse victims. Expert estimates of child abuse range from one out of every two hundred children each year to one out of forty, a gap so large as to make one think such statistics are meaningless. No wonder Mrs. Pride speaks of "marshmallow" statistics on child abuse.[5] The same is true about the statistics on missing children. The bubble has apparently been burst on this topic after we had been subjected to a veritable barrage of photographs of missing children which created the impression that millions had disappeared. Exposés in

---

Neglect and Abuse Reporting. Denver: 1984, p. 2, cited in Pride, Mary, *The Child Abuse Industry* (Westchester, IL: Crossway, 1986), p. 225.

   [4]*Ibid.*, p. 230.

   [5]*Ibid.*, pp. 24-25. Her quote is from an article which appeared in the *St. Joseph (MO) News-Press*, Sept. 18, 1985.

newspapers and on television news showed that most missing minors were either runaways or had been "snatched" by divorced parents who had failed to get custody of them. It even came to light that the reason so much attention was given to the problem in the first place was that some divorced spouses got together and decided to exploit national concern about stranger kidnappings by getting pictures of their children, after they were taken by their ex-mates, hung up all over.[6] A couple of years ago, the FBI estimated that, across America, there were only *68 cases* of missing young children whose safety was seriously feared for as a result of their abduction.[7]

Another fact about the statistics regarding child abuse needs to be made clear. This is that, of the actual abuse that *does* occur, a very small percentage — contrary to the impression created in the media — is perpetrated by natural parents, especially when both parents are present in the home. Mrs. Pride presents some instructive statistics — gotten from raw data, not the "guestimates" of most reporting on the subject — about this. As far as fatalities from child abuse are concerned, there are only about one thousand in the U.S. each year which result from the behavior of parents or guardians. This is only about one percent of all the deaths of youths under age nineteen. Frequently, the perpetrator in these fatality cases will be referred to as a "parent" or "guardian" but will actually be neither; he or she will be a paramour or live-in boyfriend.[8] (It is worth noting that government child abuse statistics do not distinguish, say, natural from foster parents, and the government is very loose in its definition of a "family.") According to one study of such cases, most of the victims came from single-parent families.[9] Actually,

---

[6]*Ibid.*, pp. 29, 235.

[7]Hippler, Arthur E., "Missing Children?" *The Wanderer*, March 6, 1986, p. 13.

[8]Pride, pp. 33, 236.

[9]*Ibid.*, p. 236. The fatality study Mrs. Pride discusses was reported in the *St. Louis Post-Dispatch* (Oct. 30, 1985) and involved 33 cases.

murder of minors by parties other than parents annually claims more than three times as many minors' lives as child abuse does.[10]

The story is much the same with sexual abuse. Even though the media and professionals involved in combating child abuse convey the impression that sexual assaults within households are an epidemic, the truth is otherwise. Incest, the most obvious form of sexual abuse of minors, is rare in intact families. Mrs. Pride states that "the vast majority of sexual abuse [incest and otherwise] occurs in non-families or broken families" and the "profile of the typical perpetrator [is] promiscuous, often remarried and more often not married (i.e., a live-in boyfriend), alcoholic, often with a criminal record."[11] The statistics do not distinguish between whether those in a household who commit sexual abuse are natural parents or not, however, so the family is left looking like a much more abusive environment than it really is. Another factor that is worth noting here is the vague, open-ended definition of "sexual abuse" (I discuss the imprecise definition of what constitutes child abuse in most statutes below), which includes "'anything from fondling [which could be simply touching a baby's private parts when powdering him or her during a diaper change] to actual sexual intercourse.'" People

---

Paramours or live-in boyfriends were involved in 15 of these and three of them had prior criminal records. Nine of the families had had a history of violence and almost 40 percent had had problems with drug or alcohol abuse or mental illness.

[10]Pride, p. 35, citing statistical tables.

[11]*Ibid.*, p. 36. She refers to other sources in backing this up, one of which is a social work text which says the following: "'step/adoptive/foster parents . . . [are] associated with the greatest frequency of sexual maltreatment . . . nonrelative and step/adoptive/foster parents are . . . often associated with sexual abuse. Almost half of the children [who were found to be sexually abused in studies] were living with a single, unemployed female caretaker.'" (Mayhall, Pamela D. and Norgard, Katherine Eastlack, *Child Abuse and Neglect: Sharing Responsibility* [New York: John Wiley & Sons, 1983], p. 11, cited in Pride, p. 237.)

have actually been accused of being, and "substantiated" as, sexual abusers for doing entirely innocent things.[12]

Why Overreporting?

Why is there so much overreporting about child abuse? Why are there so many unfounded complaints and so many people accused? One reason is the near hysteria that has been created about this subject in the last years. This has led to people reporting meaningless acts and suspicions as child abuse. The public has been encouraged by authorities to report child abuse, without their making clear exactly what "child abuse" is and, in some cases, their telling the public to report acts which clearly are *not* abuse.[13] Moreover, the initiation of child abuse hotlines, with which people can make anonymous reports, has led to more spurious reporting and to deliberate and malicious false reporting.[14] Another factor in the reporting epidemic, as

---

[12]Pride, p. 37. The quote she gives on the sexual abuse definition is from the *Nevada (MO) Daily Mail*, June 26, 1985.

[13]Consider, for example, the Illinois case where a senior citizen group, on a tour of a police station, was told they could help the authorities find out about incest by watching out for parents *hugging and kissing* their children. (Mentioned in Whitfield, Donna, "Tyranny Masquerades as Charity: Who Are the Real Child Abusers?" *Fidelity* [February 1985], p. 25.)

[14]Almost every hotline report is investigated; there is no attempt to sift out suspicious reports at that stage and the false reporter faces no liability. Mrs. Pride recounts instances of malicious reporting in her book. I personally have been told of two cases of false, utterly malicious anonymous phone reports, although at least one of these did not involve one of the new hotlines but just a call to the social service agency. One of these was in Texas, where a mixed Caucasian-Asian Indian couple was reported for allowing their infant to run unsupervised in the street. When the agency investigators discovered the child was too young to walk, it was concluded that the report was motivated by racial prejudice. The other was in Ohio, where a person — it was later concluded a hostile relative — reported a couple for

mentioned above, is that child abuse has become a favorite charge made by warring spouses in custody proceedings. It is sometimes said that alleging child abuse — especially sexual abuse — is the best way to get custody nowadays in our divorce-saturated nation, and to insure the other former mate will be denied visitation rights or joint custody.[15] Finally, several aspects about the child abuse laws, and especially changes made in them in recent years, are responsible for overreporting. I begin my discussion of these next.

Defining Abuse: The Laws

The first problem with the laws is that they are hopelessly vague in their definition — if they provide one at all — of "child abuse" and "neglect." An oft-quoted passage from Jeanne M. Giovannoni and Rosina M. Becerra's book *Defining Child Abuse* expresses this well:

> Many assume that since child abuse and neglect are against the law, somewhere there are statutes that make clear distinctions between what is and what is not child abuse and

---

permitting their baby to be malnourished. The social worker, upon seeing a plump, healthy baby, decided the complaint was false.

[15]Cases of this happening are cropping up in various publications. Mrs. Pride discusses it (Pride, pp. 54, 239). Other sources the author has seen mention it are Slicker, p. 16, and *U.S. News and World Report*, Vol. 98 (April 1, 1985), p. 66. Mrs. Pride quotes from a Missouri House of Representatives Report of testimony about false child abuse reporting, which says (p. 66 of Report): "'It is clear that parents and lawyers have determined that the only way to deny permanent visiting privileges of another spouse is to allege child abuse or sexual abuse.'" (Quoted in Pride, p. 239.)

neglect, but this is not the case. Nowhere are there clear-cut definitions of what is encompassed by the terms.[16]

Let us consider some statutes as examples. We can start with the federal "Child Abuse and Prevention Act" of 1974 which became a model for state legislation because, in order to receive federal funds under the Act, states had to bring their statutes into compliance with it. It defined "abuse" and "neglect" to mean "physical or mental injury, sexual abuse, negligent treatment, or maltreatment of a child under the age of eighteen." It did not spell out what "mental injury," "negligent treatment," or "maltreatment" is.[17]

The state statutes, following the federal model, are similar. Mrs. Pride writes about the vagueness of the statute in her home state of Missouri. It gets even broader and less precise than "mental injury" by speaking of "emotional abuse," which some authorities lump even scolding into. It also defines "neglect" as "failure to provide, by those responsible for the care, custody, and control of the child, the proper or necessary support, education as required by law, or medical, surgical, *or any other care necessary for his well-being*."[18] This entire provision is imprecise, but the last phrase, as Mrs. Pride points out, is particularly vague. She asks: "Does 'well-being' mean four weeks at camp, or a small family size, or designer jeans, or a middle class house?"[19] Obviously, when the law does not spell out the meaning of such a term, the people administering and enforcing the law attach the meaning to it they wish.

Other states are not much better. Let us take Ohio as an example. The Ohio statutes include within the term "neglected child" any child "[w]ho lacks proper parental care because of the

---

[16]Giovannoni, Jeanne M. and Becerra, Rosina M., *Defining Child Abuse* (NY: Macmillan [Free Press], 1979), p. 2.

[17]Pride, pp. 226-227.

[18]*Ibid.*, p. 227. The emphasis is not in the statute, but is provided by Mrs. Pride.

[19]*Ibid.*

faults or habits of his parents, guardian, or custodian," or "[w]hose parents, guardian, or custodian neglects or refuses to provide him with proper or necessary subsistence, education, medical or surgical care, or other care necessary for his health, morals or well-being," or "[w]hose parents, guardian, or custodian neglects or refuses to provide the special care made necessary by his mental condition."[20]   Further, the statutes define a "child without proper parental care" as one "whose home is filthy and unsanitary; whose parents, stepparents, guardian, or custodian permit him to become dependent, neglected, abused, or delinquent; whose parents, stepparents, guardians, or custodian, when able, refuse or neglect to provide him with necessary care, support, medical attention, and educational facilities; or . . . fail to subject . . . [him] to necessary discipline."[21]   What is "proper parental care?" What is meant when "the faults or habits of his parents," *et al.* is spoken of? The statute does not tell us. It is not outlandish to think that a state agency, social worker, or juvenile court judge might interpret "improper parental care" to mean being too "rigid," or methodical, or disciplined. In his paper, Robert J. D'Agostino tells us of a court case which did exactly this. (Some of the things Mrs. Pride says below that agencies view as indications of abuse make one think entirely outrageous interpretations are indeed sometimes given to such terms.) What is "proper or necessary subsistence?" Clothing which keeps up with the latest styles (designer jeans again)? Will someone in authority say one has too much sugar in his child's diet? Too little? What standards are to be applied to determine what a "proper or necessary education" is? What about home education, an increasingly popular practice but one still not widely familiar to people and generally disliked by the educational establishment? Mrs. Pride speaks of a case in Missouri where parents, both of whom were certified teachers and who had

---

[20]*Baldwin's Ohio Rev. Code Annotated*, Sec. 2151.03 (1986 Cum. Service), Vol. 3.
   [21]*Ibid.*

received the permission of local school authorities, were charged with "educational neglect" under the child abuse statute when they started a home education program for their son in association with a Christian academy. Among the objections of the state agency was that the program was "too religiously centered" and it argued that his "behavior or associations [Christian?] . . . were injurious to his welfare."[22] In another case in a suburban Philadelphia county, a poor, semi-retarded woman was in danger of having her six children taken away because authorities said — despite seeming to acknowledge she was a "loving, giving mother" — she was guilty of "emotional and intellectual neglect" because of her condition. This prompted her attorney to object that "'you can't yank kids out of what would be considered a lower class home to put them on the Mainline [an affluent, and in parts even exclusive, suburban Philadelphia area], just so they'll get into Harvard.'"[23] Indeed, isn't this the very sort of meaning we can expect some to give to vague laws? What about the "medical and surgical care" provision of the Ohio law? The statute nowhere states what this is to include. Pediatricians are generally required to report cases of "suspected abuse" to authorities. What, under this definition, would stop a pediatrician from saying such care is being withheld if a parent refuses to go along with his recommendation for some elective surgical procedure? What about the mother who refuses to accept a prescription for vitamins for a newborn because she insists on ecologically breastfeeding him (i.e., breastfeeding without any supplements)? Most pediatricians today don't seem to understand ecological breastfeeding — which provides all the nutrition a baby needs so long as the mother eats well herself and

---

[22]Pride, p. 232, quoting from the *St. Louis Globe Democrat*, March 16-17, 1985, p. 1. The story apparently received considerable discussion in St. Louis area newspapers and the *Globe-Democrat* criticized the state agency in editorials about it on April 27-28, 1985 (Pride, p. 232).

[23]"A Mother's Fight," *Philadelphia Inquirer*, Wed., Jan. 15, 1986, pp. 1-B, 4-B.

gets sufficient vitamins — so might they not conclude that necessary care is being denied in such a case? As far as the term "well being" is concerned, the same observations Mrs. Pride makes above about Missouri's law are applicable to Ohio's. What is a "filthy and unsanitary" home? Might not social workers have different views of this depending on how fastidious they are? Finally, what is "necessary discipline," and, perhaps more importantly, what are the limits to it? We consider this next in looking at Ohio's statutory definition of the term "child abuse."

Under the Ohio statute, an "abused child" is one who, *inter alia*, "[i]s the victim of 'sexual activity,' ... [i]s endangered ... [or e]xhibits evidence of any injury or death, inflicted other than by accidental means . . .," except that a child who has received corporal punishment "or other physical disciplinary measure" by a parent *et al.*, "is not an abused child."[24] A "dependent child," under the statute, is a "homeless or destitute" child or one "without proper care or support, through no fault of his parents," *et al.*, or one "[w]ho lacks proper care or support by reason of the mental or physical condition of his parents," *et al.*, or one "[w]hose condition or environment is such as to warrant the state, in the interest of the child, in assuming his guardianship."[25] There is another section of the statute which speaks about a child who "is without proper parental care or guardianship." It defines such a child, *inter alia*, as one "whose home is filthy and unsanitary; whose parents [*et al.*] ... permit him to become ... delinquent [etc.] ... whose parents ... [*et al.*] ... when able, refuse or neglect to provide him with necessary care, support [etc.] ... or ... fail to subject such child to necessary discipline...."[26] The state is permitted to take children away from their parents or guardians for any of these reasons or the reasons in the above paragraphs.

---

[24]*Baldwin's, ibid.*, Sec. 2151.03.
[25]*Ibid.*, Sec. 2151.04.
[26]*Ibid.*, Sec. 2151.05.

The vagueness and uncertainty of the statute's provisions should be apparent just by reading them. Let me comment on the troublesome nature of some of these points, however. Another part of the Ohio code is referred to in order to define what is meant by a child being "endangered." When we look at that section, we find that the exception for corporal or other physical punishment above is placed somewhat in doubt. The second provision does not permit parents, guardians, *et al.*, to:

> Administer corporal punishment or other physical disciplinary measure, or physically restrain the child in a cruel manner or for a prolonged period, which punishment, discipline, or restraint is excessive under the circumstances and creates a substantial risk of serious physical harm to the child;
> [or]
> Repeatedly administer unwarranted disciplinary measures to the child, when there is a substantial risk that such conduct, if continued, will seriously impair or retard the child's mental health or development.[27]

What standard is used to determine if the punishment is "excessive under the circumstances and creates a substantial risk?" What guarantee is there that it won't be merely the opinion of the social worker or other agency or enforcement official? Similarly, what are "unwarranted disciplinary measures" and what does "repeatedly" mean, and who decides? How does one judge the likelihood of serious impairment of such nebulous notions as "mental health" and "development"? Exactly what is "development"? It seems that Ohio law is willing to allow mere psychological constructs and theories to be the ground for depriving children of their parents, even though psychology is a highly imprecise discipline full of conflicting opinions and not

---

[27]*Ibid.*, Sec. 2919.22.

generally grounded today on a solid understanding of the nature of man.[28]

As far as being a "dependent child" is concerned, we might ask what is "proper care and support"? What does "in the interests of the child" mean? The term "support," particularly, has become a psychological "buzz word" — everybody is looking for "support" these days: emotional support, support groups, the support of an analyst. If the term was once clearly understood in statutes like this one as referring to sufficient financial support to provide the necessities for a decent upbringing, it now can be used to beat parents over the head because they believe in rebuking and punishing their children when they do something wrong, instead of just giving "positive reinforcement." As much of the rest of the discussion in this paper shows, vague terms such as these will be defined arbitrarily by state agencies and their caseworkers, often to the detriment of parents.

Similarly, a statute that leaves terms such as a child's "constitution" and "environment" up for grabs invites abuse. What constitutes a "filthy and unsanitary home" is certainly a matter of opinion: for some it is utter squalor, for others — including some zealous social workers — it could mean a little dust left on the coffee table. An example of such an unreasonable insistence on cleanliness was seen in the case of the semi-retarded suburban Philadelphia woman mentioned above.[29] Parenthetically, under the Ohio statute, parents like her are disadvantaged from the start in trying to keep their offspring

---

[28]See, for example, Kilpatrick, William Kirk, *Psychological Seduction* (Nashville: Thomas Nelson, 1983).

[29]The news report seems to indicate this. See *Philadelphia Inquirer*, *ibid.*, p. 4-B. Mrs. Pride indicates that social workers make unreasonable, extreme demands regarding cleanliness on parents frequently enough, sometimes apparently as an excuse to accuse them of something when a (probably false) hotline report has been made. See Pride, p. 160.

because of the provision about parents' "mental or physical condition."

As for the provisions about permitting a child to become delinquent and not providing "necessary discipline," two observations are in order: first, social workers are essentially given the go-ahead to decide what "necessary discipline" is both as regards results and methods, and, second, certain parts of the group of statutory provisions regarding corporal punishment discussed above may well undermine the efforts of parents to provide it.

Defining Child Abuse: Agencies and Social Workers

As a result of the vagueness of child abuse statutes, governmental social service agencies frequently have no definite guidelines on what "abuse" and "neglect" are and leave it up to individual social workers to decide. As Besharov states: "Existing standards set no limits on intervention and provide no guidelines for decision-making. They are a prime reason for the system's inability to protect obviously endangered children, even as it intervenes into family life on a massive scale."[30] Richard Gelles, a leading academic guru for family intervention advocates whose studies of family violence have been very influential in creating a picture of the family as pathologically sick, admits the following about the relativity of what is "child abuse":

> ". . . child abuse" defies logical and precise scientific definition. Malnourishment, sexual abuse, failure to feed and clothe a child, beating a child, torturing a child, withholding medical care from a child, allowing a child to live in a "deprived or depraved" environment, and helping a child stay out of school have all been defined at various times as "child abuse." The definition . . . varies over time,

---

[30]Besharov, p. 570.

across cultures, and between different social and cultural groups.[31]

Exactly how relative the definition of "child abuse" is among social workers, who are largely in charge of administering the laws, is seen in sources cited by Mrs. Pride. In two Missouri publications — one an official publication of the state's Division of Family Services and the other prepared under a grant from the Division and the U.S. Department of Health and Human Services — the following situations are mentioned (in the case of the first group) as a basis for agency intervention into a family and (in the case of the second) as reasons parents had their children taken away from them: a. neglected appearance, overneatness, child's disruptive behavior, passive or withdrawn behavior, parents being critical of the child, and isolated families "'who don't share in school or community activities.'" b. "'inadequate parenting skills,'" "'emotional neglect,'" "'unspecified neglect'" (this means neglect other than the nonprovision of shelter, nutrition, medical care, or education), "'lack of supervision,'" and "'emotional abuse or neglect.'"[32] In the Giovannoni and Becerra work mentioned above — also cited by Mrs. Pride — there is discussion of a survey of social workers and other professionals involved in child abuse reporting and enforcement which asked them to rate on a scale from 1 to 9 whether they believed various kinds of parental behaviors were

---

[31]Gelles, Richard, "A Profile of Violence Toward Children in the United States," in Gerbner, G., Ross, C., and Zigler, E., eds., *Child Abuse: An Agenda for Action* (New York: Oxford U. Press, 1980), quoted in Besharov, p. 573.

[32]Pride, pp. 60-61, 68-69. The points grouped under "a" are found in *What Everyone Should Know About Child Abuse* (Jefferson City, MO: Missouri Division of Family Services, 1976, 1980), pp. 8-9; those under "b" are found in *Foster Family Care in Missouri: An Assessment*, p. 111. This publication was prepared by the Missouri Coalition on Foster Care, an organization affiliated with the Missouri Association for Social Welfare, under a grant from the Missouri Division of Family Services and the U.S. Department of Health and Human Services.

"abusive or neglectful" (1 was least serious, 9 the most). These were some of the average ratings given by the social workers:

1. spanking with a leather strap
    (leaving red marks)   6.15

2. spanking with the hand
    (leaving red marks)   3.21

3. regularly left child alone outside the home
    during the day until almost dark   4.42

4. #3, if neighbors have spotted the child
    wandering five blocks from home   5.33

5. regularly left the child alone inside
    the house after dark   6.33

6. constantly screaming at the child,
    calling him foul names   5.19

7. ignoring child most of time   5.57

8. never require children to do homework,
    letting them watch TV all evening,
    and one child is failing   4.23[33]

---

[33]*Ibid.*, p. 230, citing Giovannoni and Becerra, pp. 111-121. It is interesting to note that no social worker gave any of the behaviors a "1" (this score indicates, essentially, the belief that no abuse nor neglect was present). The survey appears to have been done in the latter half of the 1970s.

Two points are important about these survey results. The first is that none of these behaviors is a clear-cut case of abuse or neglect; at best, some are only arguably so. Some are not abusive or neglectful at all, according to any commonsensical standard. The second is that it illustrates conflicting views among social workers themselves. Even they — the ones most involved in enforcing the laws — have no certain definition of these terms. This study closely comported with another cited by Besharov which showed that persons working in child protective agencies around the country — in areas covering the majority of the American population — believed "'it is difficult to say what is and what is not child maltreatment.'"[34] The result of this, according to

---

[34]Besharov, pp. 569-570, citing a national survey of local child abuse programs done in the first half of the 1970s (Nagi, Saad Z., "Child Abuse and Neglect Programs: A National Overview," *Children Today*, Vol. 4, No. 3 [May-June 1975], p. 17). We should not be surprised that some social workers regard such innocent parental behaviors as spanking as "child abuse." They are trained in the colleges and universities by academic theorists — sociologists, psychologists, etc. — some of whom, as Mrs. Pride indicates, have gone on a crusade to treat spanking as exactly that and to bring about its criminalization and abolition. See, for example, Pride, pp. 30-31, discussing the views of Murray A. Straus, Richard J. Gelles, and Suzanne K. Steinmetz in their book, *Behind Closed Doors: Violence and the American Family* (Garden City, NY: Doubleday [Anchor], 1980). Gelles, particularly, has been a very influential writer-academic on family issues. Another major work says the following about the thinking expressed in this book and shows how widely shared it is among academics who study the family: "Many analysts . . . agree that another contributing factor in child abuse is a relatively high tolerance for violence in our society [the Straus, Gelles, and Steinmetz book is cited as one of the sources, but from what she says they are only a few of the many analysts] . . . For example, the acceptance of corporal punishment throughout society, without any clear sanctions against its excessive use, or even any clear distinctions between how much is acceptable and how much is excessive, can be seen as a source of potential child abuse rooted in societal values." Giovannoni, Jeanne M., "Child Abuse and Neglect: An Overview," in Laird, Joan and Hartman, Ann, eds., *A Handbook of Child Welfare*

Besharov, is that "[e]xisting standards set no limits on intervention and provide no guidelines for decision-making."[35] Social workers can remove children from their homes for no certain reason and without evidence of their having been harmed or being in danger. They can avoid having to get prior permission from a court to do so and are often able to delay the hearings required by law after they take custody of the children.[36]

The same confusion about what child abuse and neglect are affects physicians and hospitals, who are required by law to report "suspected" cases. In the study Besharov discusses above, an even higher percentage of physicians than social workers were unclear about what constituted "child maltreatment." The media and different publications reported a 1982 case in which parents took their baby to St. Louis's Cardinal Glennon Hospital at their physician's suggestion to find out why the infant was spitting up so much. The hospital found no physical problem and arbitrarily accused the parents of "emotional neglect" (which hospital officials admitted they could not define).[37] I personally have been told of a case of parents taking a small child to the emergency room at a Boston hospital because of a skin problem that suddenly developed. Physicians at the hospital insisted it was a burn — which they decided was inflicted by the parents — and said they were going to file a child abuse report

---

(NY: Macmillan [Free Press], 1985), p. 195. Every parent using corporal punishment, then, is seen as a potential or actual abuser.

[35]Besharov, p. 570.

[36]Mrs. Pride reports on a study in Missouri which showed that 45 percent of the children taken from their parents and placed in foster care did not have a hearing on their cases for over twelve months after their removal. (Pride, p. 68, citing *Foster Family Care in Missouri: An Assessment*, p. 106.)

[37]See Bresharov, pp. 569-570 for the information on the study he cites. The St. Louis hospital case is discussed in Whitfield, p. 24 and Pride, p. 233. According to Pride, the case was reported on Jack Anderson's radio program on Nov. 27-28, 1982. The hospital reported this "emotional abuse" to the authorities who then proceeded to regularly check up on and monitor the family as suspected abusers.

with authorities. The parents, acting quickly, went to out-of-town physicians who confirmed the misdiagnosis: the problem was no burn at all. The hospital, fearing legal action, acknowledged its error and promised to appoint a committee to consider a new policy for making determinations about child abuse cases.

Judges, likewise, do not seem to know what "abuse" or "neglect" are. The survey Besharov cites above along with various court opinions, indicate they judge these cases according to the context of the circumstances. As Besharov observes, they "are saying that, although they cannot define child maltreatment, they know it when they see it."[38]

So much for the vagueness in the meaning of "child abuse." Let us consider other problems with the child abuse statutes which have contributed to the large number of unfounded allegations. We have already mentioned the lack of legal restrictions on agencies' removal of children from the home and on the provision of expeditious hearings. One of the other problems is the fact that the federal statute which, as noted, spawned the tougher state laws, requires a state to "provide for the reporting of known and *suspected* instances of child abuse and neglect,"[39] if it wishes to receive federal funds — usually a great lure that states seldom forego. This provision has resulted in state laws which mandate that professionals and anyone working with children — some states require anyone *at all* — report even suspected cases of abuse (without ever defining it clearly, as noted).[40] Many of these cases of suspected abuse, as we have seen, are really no abuse at all.

Besides the requirement for reports based only on suspicions — whatever they may be — as a prerequisite to

---

[38]Besharov, pp. 568-569. See these pages for the citation of some current court cases.

[39]Child Abuse and Prevention Act (Pub. L. 93-247, Sec. 4 [6] [2] [C] — later 42 U.S.C., Sec. 5103), cited in Besharov, p. 543, n. 19. Emphasis added by this writer.

[40]See Pride, pp. 14, 228.

receiving funds, the federal Child Abuse and Prevention Act also mandated that a state statute "include provisions for immunity for persons reporting instances of child abuse and neglect from prosecution . . . arising out of such reporting."[41] States went even a step further than this, guaranteeing not only immunity from prosecution — which is generally interpreted to refer to the filing of criminal charges — but also immunity from civil liability for required reporters, state social service employees, and even, in some cases, anonymous hotline complainants. The "good faith" of reporters is presumed under many of these statutes. What the state statutes also do, however, is to threaten with civil and, in some cases, criminal liability any mandated reporter who does not make a report when he is "suspicious."[42]

Other Aspects of the Laws and the Rights of the Accused

Another aspect about the current statutes is that they provide little protection for the constitutional rights of the accused, which is especially outrageous in light of the large majority of those accused who appear to be innocent. Mrs. Pride compiles helpful data about the civil rights of those accused of child abuse in each of the fifty states. She considers which states guarantee five basic due process rights generally given in criminal cases: the right to be informed of the charge while under investigation, the right to trial by jury, access to records being

---

[41]*Supra*, n. 28, Sec. 4 (b) (2) (A) of the Act.

[42]Among the problems this has created is a breakdown of the traditional relationships of confidentiality between private physicians, therapists, and other professionals and their patients. A corollary problem has been that some people who genuinely need help in dealing with their children and either might become abusers or are engaging in some of the vague, borderline behaviors discussed earlier are dissuaded from seeking it. See Whitfield, p. 25; Pride, pp. 55-56.

kept on the person, the right to have an unsubstantiated record removed or not to have a record placed in a file until after a hearing, and the right to challenge information in one's record. Persons accused of child abuse — most of whom are parents — have none of these rights in thirty-one states. Some states guarantee one or more of these rights; none protects all of them. None of the fifty states requires that the accused be told of the charges, only one permits a person to request a jury trial, sixteen permit access to records under at least some conditions, fourteen protect against unsubstantiated records being kept in the file at least as a general rule, and fourteen permit challenges to the record.[43] Another aspect of due process which is not upheld in child abuse proceedings is the right to appeal, provided in state statutes for both criminal and civil matters.[44] As Mrs. Pride writes, even if on paper one has a right to appeal civil matters such as decisions in child abuse proceedings, he may not be able to effectively pursue that appeal. Appellate courts seldom make their own fact findings; normally they accept the facts as determined at a trial court or hearing (in child abuse matters, it is usually a civil hearing) and will just consider questions of law. The rub here is that in child abuse proceedings one has no right to review the record in most states, as has been noted, and in fact, no evidence upon which to base an appeal may even have been presented at the initial hearing. Recall that state agencies really do not need evidence to conclude that abuse has occurred or to take away children or impose other sanctions, and hearing judges are generally not required to solicit it.[45]

---

[43]Pride, p. 169. It appears that she is reporting on the state of the laws as of 1984.

[44]State statutes do not necessarily guarantee the right of appeal but they establish procedures and mechanics for it and, at least in criminal matters, are rather liberal in practice in allowing appeals to be filed and heard. One Pennsylvania attorney told me that appeals in both criminal and civil matters nowadays are routine.

[45]Pride, p. 229.

A further fact about the constitutional rights of those accused of child abuse is that guarantees of the Fourth Amendment against unreasonable search and seizure do not apply. We have already seen the wide latitude social workers have in removing children from their homes even without evidence of abuse; this in itself is a "search and seizure." Also, once let into a home — in some states, when accompanied by a policeman, a social worker can force entry; often, however, they secure entry even when not entitled to do so by making threats or because parents do not know they have a right to refuse — a social worker has virtually *carte blanche* to look around for anything to build a case against parents. They can even strip a child and do body cavity searches to find evidence of sexual abuse.[46] No warrant is required for any of this; the statutes usually permit authorities to circumvent judicial approval for their actions or for taking custody of a child if they believe the child to be imminently in danger (without usually defining what this means).

One will probably wonder how such basic rights can be ignored in child abuse cases. The reason is that, as noted, most child abuse investigations do not involve the criminal law. Child abuse is mostly dealt with under state juvenile statutes which are civil matters, but civil matters of a special type. Due to the

---

[46]*Ibid.*, pp. 160-161, 228-229. Cases of such invasive searches of children's bodies have been recounted in some of the literature. See Pride, p. 228; Whitfield, pp. 25, 26; Besharov, p. 557. Pride reports on a federal court decision in Illinois in 1985 — she does not give the name of the case or any indication of whether it was reported — which held that the state's Department of Children and Family Services did not have to get search warrants because the parents in question had "consented" to searches of their homes and children because they had let social workers in (despite the fact that all did so in the face of threats or in ignorance of their rights) and because searches to investigate child abuse were "reasonable" and thus could be undertaken without a warrant. The plaintiffs were parents who had been falsely accused of child abuse.

efforts of juvenile crime experts, psychologists, leaders in the social service community, *et al.*, juvenile matters generally have been distanced from the criminal law and enforcement apparatus, supposedly to avoid "traumatizing" troubled youth, to make it possible to get them on the right track before adulthood if they have been offenders, or otherwise to insure that they be protected. The juvenile justice or juvenile affairs procedures which have been set up are thereby less formal than normal court proceedings, and the usual legal rules and guarantees do not always apply.[47]

Another disturbing aspect of recent child abuse statutes — somewhat involving the restriction of procedural guarantees — is that they almost automatically assume the truth of a child's allegations and testimony against the accused. This has resulted not only in false charges, but has also left children easily subject to manipulation by prosecutorial and social service agency authorities and has promoted the driving of a wedge between children and their parents. Some of the legal changes in question here — for the cases that actually do get to court — are the changing of courtroom hearsay rules to permit out-of-court videotape testimony by children, abolishing the minimum ages below which children are presumed to be incompetent to testify, and eliminating the need for corroborating a child's testimony. Along with these have been questionable new practices developed by child therapists and child abuse investigators in order to ostensibly get the correct story from allegedly victimized children. These have included excessive and suggestive questioning and the use of dolls with disproportionately large private parts to supposedly help the child express that he or she was sexually abused. Many authorities strongly criticize the use of such dolls as being highly unreliable.[48] A further problem with interrogating children is simply that — as anyone who knows

---

[47]A few of these points are discussed by Pride, p. 229.
[48]See Pride, pp. 47-48.

anything about small children should realize — they get things confused, they do not always understand the implications of what they say, and they sometimes make up stories. A good example of the responses that can be elicited from suggestive interrogation of children in an abuse investigation is seen in an account of the Jordan, Minnesota nightmare in 1983-84 when 24 people, mostly parents, were falsely accused of child sexual abuse by a seemingly ruthless, politically ambitious county prosecutor. Investigators, according to one person's account, would ask five-year-olds, "'Did your mommy or daddy hurt you?' Well, hurt to them was a spanking or something on that order, and that's how they proceeded after that."[49]

The reason such legal changes have been enacted is because of what Mrs. Pride calls "the doctrine of the immaculate confession."[50] In their college and other professional training nowadays, social workers are taught that children simply *do not lie or falsify*, especially when telling about child abuse.[51] As noted above, it is clear, in general, that children do not always tell the truth. On the matter of children not lying about abuse, particularly sexual abuse, the Institute for Psychological Therapies says bluntly: "'[t]here is no empirical evidence to support this claim. There have been no controlled studies to test it.'"[52] An interesting, seemingly contradictory, corollary to this

---

[49]Jones, E. Michael, "Abuse Abuse: The Therapeutic State Terrorizes Parents in Jordan, Minnesota," *Fidelity* (Feb. 1985), p. 28, quoting one of the falsely accused parents, a local policeman. This article is a good, brief account of the Jordan affair.

[50]Pride, p. 44.

[51]Wakefield, Hollida and Underwager, Ralph, unpublished manuscript on the child witness and sexual abuse, Institute for Psychological Therapies, quoted in Slicker, p. 18. See also Pride, pp. 44, 48.

[52]Wakefield and Underwager, quoted in Slicker, *ibid*. Accounts of children and adolescents lying about their being victims of child abuse frequently appear in the literature about overreporting. This is just a sampling: a foster father was accused falsely of abuse by a street-wise teenage girl he took in because he wouldn't let her go on overnight

doctrine of the immaculate confession is that if a child, in spite of suggestions from interrogators, denies he was ever abused, or if he makes an accusation and later recants it, his denials or recantations are supposed to be discounted. In Missouri, this dubious corollary has even been enshrined into the law. The child abuse statute was changed there to allow a child's earlier statements to be introduced in court against an accused person even if the child later retracted them. The rationale for this was that he might change his statements if he is pressured by his parents or other persons accused.[53] The law seems odd in that, if the charge of abuse is particularly serious, the child will be kept from the alleged perpetrator before trial anyhow, and, while acknowledging the possibility of the accused influencing the child's story, it completely ignores the possibility of police, social service agency, or prosecutorial influence.

Another corollary of the immaculate confession doctrine is something called the "Child Sexual Abuse Accommodation Syndrome," which holds the following: 1) sexually abused children tend to contradict themselves; 2) sexually abused children cover up the incident; 3) sexually abused children often show no emotion after the event; and 4) sexually abused children often wait a long time before making their accusations. As Mrs. Pride says about such criteria, "all the evidence typically used to

---

dates (Pride, pp. 21, 232); in Maryland, a girl who had alleged abuse was later shown to have made up the story by repeating in detail a television serial plot about an abused youth to authorities (*U.S. News and World Report, op. cit.*); two boys alleged to police that they had been kidnapped by a man they described in detail — it was later discovered they had made up the story just to torment their parents who they were angry with (Goodman, Gail, "The Child Witness: Conclusions and Future Directions for Research and Legal Practice," *Jour. of Social Issues*, Vol. 40 [1984], pp. 158, 164, 165, quoted in Slicker, p. 16).

[53]Pride, p. 44.

show no sexual abuse occurred . . . has now been captured to prove the very opposite!"[54]

Children Threatened by Current Laws and Practices

In considering the new laws, with much tighter mandatory reporting requirements, grounds for much more state intervention into families, and the permitting of unchallenged child testimony, it is natural to ask this question: Are they succeeding in protecting children from real abuse? Many sources say they are inadequate, partly *because* of the overreporting and overintervention they encourage. Besharov states the following:

> Th[e] high level of state intervention might be acceptable if it were necessary to enable child protective agencies to fulfill their basic mission of protecting endangered children. Unfortunately, it does just the opposite; children in real danger of serious maltreatment get lost in the press of the minor cases flooding the system.[55]

In other words, as Mrs. Pride puts it, "If *all* parents are guilty, or could be guilty," — which seems to be the upshot of the current child abuse laws and agency attitudes — "then resources end up spread thinly. There is no way to separate the criminals from the average Joes. . . . A system that fails to distinguish crimes from unfashionable child-rearing practices cannot protect children."[56] After all, state agencies have only so many personnel — they frequently complain that they are understaffed and overworked,

---

[54]*Ibid.*, p. 46. One psychiatrist, testifying for the prosecution in a well-publicized child sexual abuse case in California involving a state official — it was a false allegation of abuse — admitted under cross-examination that a child who had not been abused might behave in exactly the same way. (Pride, p. 240, citing Kirp, David L., "Hug Your Kid, Go to Jail," *American Spectator* [June 1985], p. 33.)

[55]Besharov, p. 562.

[56]Pride, p. 55.

even while justifying more and more intervention into families —
and funds do not flow so freely in a period of governmental belt
tightening.[57] The unprecedentedly high level of intervention into
families has not produced particularly impressive results in
protecting children. As an article in the leftist magazine
Progressive states, "'Of all the children believed to have died of
child abuse or neglect [in the U.S.], an estimated 25 percent were
known to child protective agencies at the time of their death.'"[58]

Another way in which current practices threaten children is
by consigning them in ever greater numbers to the troubled foster
care system — sometimes after taking them from their parents
without good cause. As with intervention into the family in the
first place "there are no legal standards governing the foster care
decision"[59] and often no time limits as to how long children
remain in what is supposed to be a "short term remedy." The
result is that children frequently are away from their parents for
years, shifted from one foster home to another.[60] This, by itself, is
one way that children can be harmed by foster care. As Besharov
states, "[l]ong-term foster care can leave lasting psychological

---

[57]Besharov says this further about the result of agency staff shortages
coupled with the overreporting problem: "Forced to allocate a
substantial portion of their limited resources to . . . 'unfounded' reports,
protective agencies often are unable to respond promptly and
effectively when children are in serious danger.

"Staff shortages limit the number and extent of investigations.
With more work than they can handle, case workers do not have
enough time to give individual cases the attention required. In the rush
to clear cases, workers often perform abbreviated investigations and
fail to discover key facts." (Besharov, p. 563.)

[58]Wexler, Richard, "Invasion of the Child Savers: No One is Safe in
the War Against Abuse," *The Progressive* (Sept. 1985), p. 22, cited in
Pride, p. 74. Besharov recounts a number of cases in which children
who had been investigated by agencies for possible abuse were not
given proper protection and were later killed or died from injuries due
to abuse. (See Besharov, pp. 551, 552, 563, 564.)

[59]Besharov, p. 584.

[60]*Ibid.*, p. 560.

scars . . . it can do irreparable damage to the bond of affection and commitment between parent and child."[61]

A more obvious way that children are harmed by foster care is when they are placed in undesirable foster homes with potentially abusive and neglectful foster parents. Mrs. Pride discusses cases of children being assaulted, neglected, and even dying in foster care and gives the startling statistic that the death rate for children placed in foster care in Florida is more than double that of children in the general population.[62] So called "emergency shelters," run by state agencies for children to be placed in immediately after removal from their homes, have also been responsible for abuse.[63] In some places, allegedly abused and neglected children are actually placed in jail or a detention center while social workers try to arrange a foster placement. There, they are faced with real danger from juvenile or adult offenders.[64]

Why Are Parental Rights Being Suppressed?

We have considered the facts about the child abuse situation and the frequently unwarranted state intrusion into families and removal of children. The question we now ask is: why? First, why do social workers and other public social service personnel have the anti-family attitudes they do, and why have laws been passed which have given such opportunities for suppression of parental rights. We can fairly accurately answer the second part of this question by answering the first part, since state agencies and social service organizations and the academic theorists backing them up have been influential in changing the laws. One basic part of the answer is in the rejection by people in

---

[61]*Ibid.*
[62]See Pride, pp. 77-79, 81.
[63]Whitfield, p. 26.
[64]Pride, pp. 81-83.

this field of the true understanding of the family and the rights
and responsibilities of parents, grounded in the natural moral
order, which Dr. Waters describes. They, for the most part,
operate from a relativistic mind-set: nothing, including the
family, exists by nature, everything is merely conventional, and
further, there are no true moral standards, so the state sets the
standards on the basis of predominant professional opinion.

Whenever some case of an agency bundling and accusing
innocent parents of abuse comes to light, its spokesmen assert
that their people erred because they lacked sufficient training.
They call for better qualified personnel and more funds to hire
them or to further train their people. The problem, however, is
not the lack of training, but the kind of learning and training they
have had. We have already seen how the training they get on at
least some specific matters relating to the determination of the
existence of child abuse — e.g., the "immaculate confession" — is
well nigh ridiculous. This is not the only problem with it,
however. Social service professionals are examples of the
"quarter-educated" people Russell Kirk speaks about who are
being turned out in droves by American colleges and
universities,[65] trained to be narrow specialists — nay, technicians
— but with hardly any liberal learning at all. This is not primarily
because of the nature of social work curricula or because they
didn't take the right courses — although this is no doubt a key
factor — but rather because of the relativistic bias of American
university education generally today. It embodies the idea either
that truth does not exist or, if it does, that it is unattainable by
human reason. This is not the only reason that social workers,
like other typical products of American education, are relativists
and thus positivists — believing that the sole determiner of right
conduct is the state — but it is probably the major one. (Some
other reasons that we could also add are the general intellectual

---

[65]The phrase is found in Kirk's *Decadence and Renewal in the Higher
Learning* (South Bend, IN: Gateway, 1978), p. xviii.

and secular environment of America today of which they are products, their lower schooling, their often liberal religious or areligious upbringing, and the social and moral biases of the middle and upper middle classes of which they are generally a part.) The very relativism of social workers, growing substantially out of their training, then, is the first reason we can point to for their anti-family, anti-parent bias.

Other reasons we can point to follow. The sexual revolution, which has deeply influenced the so-called "helping" professions (which is really quite a misnomer — How many jobs truly do not involve helping others in some way?) like social work, and college-educated persons in America generally, is a factor. This revolution holds that there are no true limits on sexual activity, that a person can choose to do what he or she wants so long as no one is "hurt." This view, of course, means that pleasure is the primary aim of such activity, and logically involves rejecting the notion that children should necessarily issue from it and taking all possible steps to make sure they don't (e.g., contraception and, if need be, abortion). If pleasure and self-gratification are the ends, one is not going to think very highly of family life with its heavy responsibilities, self-sacrifice, uncertainties, and heartaches. Children and family life often stand in the way of self-gratification. Further, if one subscribes to an ethic that makes one willing even to go to the extreme of destroying children, as with abortion, he is unlikely to have a high regard for the family which is oriented so much to protecting children. Thus, anti-family attitudes result, attitudes which are disrespectful and even disdainful of people who uphold them in both theory and practice as devoted parents do (such people are often the target of agency investigations triggered by false child abuse allegations).

Moreover, the shallowness of the sexual revolution often leads the people caught up in it — especially, one suspects, women (most social workers are women) — to a kind of envy for those who have been successful at finding the love and happiness

which has eluded them in marriage and family life. Those who
have been even more harshly victimized by the sexual revolution
— such as women whose husbands have dropped them and their
family responsibilities for some "young flame" (again,
disproportionately, women seem to be the ones affected) — also
react with envy to the latter, but it is an envy, particularly in the
person trapped in a secular mind-set, which burns to the pitch of
hatred. It is a hatred for family life and those living it prompted,
at least subconsciously, by their own failure. The latter type of
person fits Mrs. Pride's "social worker perpetrator profile": the
older, white female with poor personal home life. (This is the
social worker who thinks little of parental rights or meddling with
family integrity; it is a take-off on the "typical child abuser
profile" we hear about.) The other type of person who fits Mrs.
Pride's "social worker perpetrator profile" is "young, unmarried,
fresh out of college with no experience or significant training in
dealing with children, white middle or upper-class background."
This shows another way, usually unmentioned, about how social
workers are genuinely poorly trained for the sensitive work in the
child abuse area they do, training which no number of college
credits will provide.   Mrs. Pride tells us that "these two
descriptions fit most of the really outrageous social workers."[66]

The tendency in contemporary American life to worship
experts is another reason we can point to for unjust state
intervention into the family. Americans willingly have turned
over control and decision-making in many areas of their lives to
experts. This is partly because they have been told so frequently
and persistently that experts know better than they do about
almost everything. But this relegation of authority follows a
typical pattern: people, convinced they should do so voluntarily,
find it becomes coercive. On matters relating to the family, the
first major area that parents surrendered was education,
although here from an early point in our history coercion was

---

[66]Pride, p. 241.

used since the compulsory attendance laws quickly emerged. Coercion became tighter as time went on, however, and extended to more areas of education, such as curriculum, school standards, and teacher qualification. Now, with the child abuse laws, we have the situation where, potentially, all aspects of childrearing are scrutinized and dictated by experts with the coercive power of the state to back them up. The general willingness to defer so many things to experts, ever increasing in the twentieth century, made possible the current child abuse laws and their oppressive, anti-parent enforcement.

Closely related to this submission to experts is the nature of the bureaucratic mentality. People in government bureaucracies have a "we know best" attitude, based on their expertise. Generally, such an attitude is not merited, either in terms of their particular backgrounds and qualifications, *per se*, or in comparison to those they are regulating. This is especially the case when we are talking about the most basic areas of human endeavor, such as the rearing and education of the young.

What stands behind such bureaucratic arrogance is the statism that has pervaded the mainstream of American public opinion at least since the fourth decade of the twentieth century. Americans, supposedly in the name of promoting greater justice and a better way of life, have increasingly submitted to governmental control. Increasingly heavy regulation and regimentation has become the order of the day, to the extent that very little truly private activity remains. This began, especially, with economic activity and steadily spread to other areas, with the result that many rights that Americans in the nineteenth century would have taken for granted are hardly evident today. Reinforcing these statist and bureaucratic tendencies is a turning away from democratic attitudes on the part of so many in the college-educated element of American society. This is a pattern which people such as Mortimer Adler first noticed emerging in the 1930s,[67] but which seems to have intensified as a result of the New Left activism of the 1960s. It is very evident today in the general intolerance we witness of viewpoints outside of the relativist, leftist mainstream in the academy and in the general defense by the American left of the undemocratic courts making public policy. It is not surprising that some speakers in the symposium which generated this book spoke of current trends leading America in the direction of a "democratic totalitarianism" in which we will formally elect our leaders but with little control over the decisions and policies that are made. When social service agency people say things like "we have to stop pretending that kids have to testify [about child abuse] like adults. If all they can do is show that should be enough,"[68] and when they pursue policies like "erring on the side of the child,"[69] even when the results are false accusations against parents and suppression of their natural rights, what we see is an expression of the radical statist notion — more, the totalitarian notion — that children primarily belong to the state and not, as Dr. Waters has shown, to their parents acting in the place of God.

Why the Child Abuse Issue Has Reached a Fever Pitch Recently

A second "why" question that must be asked is this: Why have these new, repressive child abuse laws and agency enforcement practices come about *now*, and why has the child abuse hysteria occurred *now*? One reason that can probably be pointed to is that we are seeing the first generation of social workers and state bureaucrats almost completely trained in the

---

[67]See Adler, Mortimer J., *Reforming Education* (Boulder, CO: Westview, 1977).

[68]This quote is from the prosecutor in the Jordan, Minnesota case. She was quoted in *Newsweek*, and the quote appears in Jones, p. 30.

[69]See Pride, Chap. 8.

morally relativistic, anti-family, pro-statist, pro-permissive parenting views we have spoken of as taking control over state social service agencies. Those among the ranks of agency personnel who do not go along with this perspective either do not stay long — departing either voluntarily or involuntarily — or simply conform their thinking or keep their disagreements to themselves. Another reason, also relating to social service personnel, is that this is a time, because of the training of greater numbers of women in college for this field than ever and the unprecedented epidemic of divorce in America, when the number of women meeting Mrs. Pride's "social worker perpetrator profile" is at an all time high. Other reasons relate, again, to the sexual revolution and its sub-revolutions. As I have said, the sexual revolution has brought divorce. It has also brought adultery, contraceptive use (first done primarily within marriages, then by single people to "protect" themselves in their escapades, then by minors who have gotten access to it through private agencies and government behind their parent's backs), abortion (also gotten by minors in the same way), and classroom sex education as a way of providing justification for the revolution. I have already tried to show how it was logical that the sexual revolution, in general, would seek to undercut the family. Should we be surprised that the child abuse laws would be used to completely destroy parental control and authority over their children when we had already been undermining it specifically in the crucial area of the sexual and reproductive practices of children by providing them, often without parental approval, with contraception, abortion and sex education? The widespread practices of contraception and abortion have also given rise — as would be expected by their very nature — to an anti-child attitude, which easily turned into an anti-family attitude. The latter happens most readily in a secularistic, amoral environment in which the bonds of responsibility, in general, but especially in matters relating to sex and human relationships are radically loosened. This, then, had two further results, both of which fed into the child abuse issue. First, if being anti-child is the norm, and if, in fact, thousands of children are being killed by their mother's decision each week in legal abortions — and others are killed by respectable members of the medical profession in hospitals, among the most respectable institutions in our local communities, by means of infanticide shortly after birth[70] — some people, at least those most prone to violence or disregard for others or who might be prompted to such by alcohol or drugs (frequently the case in our era of amorality and meaninglessness), will engage in child abuse or neglect. This likelihood grows with people living in an ongoing arrangement with somebody else's children for whom they have no personal attachment (as is happening to a greater extent than ever as a result of the sexual revolution, with the great amount of divorce and remarriage of people with children and people cohabiting). Second, the plague of abortion and the subliminal guilt felt by many in our population about it — especially those who have had them, aided others to get them, or advocated their easy availability — has led to the child abuse hysteria. The attitude says, "let's atone for our sharing in the destruction of so many children by protecting — or so we think — some other children." It frankly is probably less of an atonement than a handy excuse for such actions and an opportunity to assuage one's guilt. The view one takes is, "I'm not so bad for having an abortion — these other people have hurt an actually born and grown child." Similarly, others who have ridden the crest of the sexual revolution and have acted irresponsibly, immorally, and have psychologically and emotionally damaged children's lives by their actions find a ready scapegoat in child abuse. As California psychologist W.R. Coulson said, "all those people who are divorced and child-abandoning really are able to steer the attention away from . . . [themselves] . . . by pointing at this awful

---

[70]See Gerry, Martin H., "The Civil Rights of Handicapped Infants: An Oklahoma 'Experiment,'" *Issues in Law and Medicine*, Vol. 1, No. 1 (July 1985), pp. 15-16.

thing [child abuse] which others do. They're able to say, 'Well, at least I'm not a child abuser. I'm only a child abandoner.'[71] Perhaps one of the reasons completely innocent, and even necessary, childrearing practices (I disagree with Dr. Rinn about this) such as spanking are made so much of by anti-child abuse activists stems from the need to create artificial monsters in order to overlook genuine ones. In a broader sense, this dismissal from moral discussion of matters which are truly immoral — usually personal matters relating to sexual morality — and the almost exclusive focus on other matters which, while perhaps having a moral dimension, are either not wrong in and of themselves or whose occurrence is only speculative or uncertain — e.g., nuclear war — is characteristic of our times.

Further, should we be so surprised in light of the sexual revolution that there are so many false reports — the ones that are of a nonmalicious nature — of child abuse? After all, the widespread use of contraception has meant that people have few or no children, and the mentality that says both parents must work means that the children that they do have are shipped off to relatives or to day care so they may never learn what childrearing necessarily involves. Since the contraceptive mentality is now a few generations old, older people cannot even remember what it was like to raise children — it was so long ago that they had their one or two — so they are easily influenced by self-serving child protective agencies to report parents for innocent actions.

Another reason why repressive child abuse laws are appearing at this time is that too many legislators have fallen under the sway of movements such as contemporary feminism, which is anti-family. It sees the family as constrictive of women and the source of archaic and oppressive attitudes toward women. It must be remembered that contemporary feminism comes out of the background of movement for sexual liberation — which as noted above, must of necessity reject the family —

---

[71]Coulson, W.R., quoted in Jones, p. 33.

and, in fact, to some degree, has given it legitimacy by wrapping itself in the cloak of high-sounding appeals to equality and rights.

A Totalitarian and Utopian Bent

There are two final observations to make about the reasons for the current state of the child abuse laws. One is that it represents the same kind of fallacious attitude seen in much of American law today — reflecting a secularized Calvinism — that all serious moral problems — at least those which the secular society chooses to define as moral — can be effectively addressed by the positive law. In fact, according to this perspective, there is no other way they *can* be addressed. I am not saying the law should not punish genuine cases of child abuse or that in very serious cases the law should not remove children from their parents' care. I *am* saying that the law is inadequate, by itself, to deal with this problem, which is, at the core, a result of people refusing to carry out moral obligations or else acting immorally — by fornicating and cohabiting, walking out on their wives, abusing drugs, alcohol, etc., (these are the practices that most commonly lead to child abuse). Law can only go so far in promoting virtue, and, in any event, the last thing any contemporary positivist will admit to doing is seeking to make people act virtuously.[72] To do this involves having to make a judgment about right and wrong which the positivist, who is also a relativist, will not do. The things that really need to be done to stop child abuse — restoring

---

[72]In fact, however, this amounts to being what the law aims to do, even if, in the official line of the relativistic social and legal thinker, this is rejected. Take the laws on race and sex discrimination, for example. They have had a considerable impact on reshaping attitudes. Indeed, the child abuse laws also are aimed at making people behave differently. It is not called making them moral or virtuous, however, but "behavior modification," or "rehabilitation," or "correcting psychological problems," or something like that.

a sense of the dignity of family life and the obligations that go along with it, replacing the ethic of sexual liberation with that of chastity, acknowledging the sanctity of innocent human life, and emphasizing the centrality of religion in peoples' lives — are either dismissed or scoffed at. The secular positivistic state tries to right everything by the civil law, oblivious to the fact that if it is genuinely serious about such an undertaking, it could accomplish it only by totalitarian, police-state repression (i.e., to control all families one would have to monitor each household closely and constantly).[73]

The other observation is that the ideology behind the child abuse laws and the actions of the enforcement agencies share the utopian character of many contemporary social and political movements. Indeed, just as the movements it is related to, those for sexual and women's "liberation," have their utopian fantasies,[74] so does the enterprise of "child advocacy." The chief,

_____

[73]St. Thomas Aquinas, in contrast to the Calvinist background the modern-day positivists unconsciously reflect, recognized that human law or the civil law is limited in matters it can deal with. He said: "Human laws do not forbid all vices, from which the virtuous abstain, but only the more grievous vices, from which it is possible for the majority to abstain. . . . Human law does not forbid all vicious acts, by obligation of a precept, as neither does it prescribe all acts of virtue." (Aquinas, *Treatise on Law, Summa Theologica*, Ques. 96, Arts. 2 and 3 [South Bend, IN: Gateway], pp. 92, 94.) The reason for this is that "it does not lay upon the multitude of imperfect men the burdens of those who are already virtuous, *viz.*, that they should abstain from all evil. Otherwise, these imperfect ones, being unable to bear such precepts, would break out into yet greater evils. . . ." (*Ibid.*, Ques. 96, Art. 2, p. 92.) Often, in the case of child abuse laws and their enforcement, as we have discussed, we actually see neither vice being repressed nor virtue promoted, but rather someone's trendy notion of childrearing being forced on someone else.

[74]The sexual liberationists believe sex can be undertaken without limits and without consequences. Women's liberationists believe that a woman can practically abandon her family and "fulfill" herself with no adverse effects on anyone. They also promote fantasies like that of "superwoman," the woman who, pursuing a career, raising a family,

unstated premise underlying the latter's thinking is — contrary to all the facts and the wisdom of the ages — that it doesn't make any difference whether children are raised in a family or not, that the family is dispensable and they can be raised just as satisfactorily by the state or any other institution.[75] Finally, there is the additional utopian belief that when a group — any group — of people is given absolute power — as has essentially been given to child abuse enforcement authorities — they won't abuse it.

Proposals for Change

What should we do about the child abuse laws and enforcement practices? There are a number of legal changes that should be made right away, even though I recognize that making them would abruptly change the direction this area of law has been going in throughout most of the country. The first step should be to eliminate the anonymous hotlines, which have been an open door to false reporting. Secondly, the laws obviously need to spell out more specifically what "child abuse" and "child neglect" are. Provisions which infringe or could be interpreted to infringe upon the parent's right to choose the childrearing

---

building a marriage, and engaging in sundry other endeavors simultaneously, can be a smashing success in them all. The truth is that some things — usually the marriage and family — suffer, and often they all do.

[75]The belief that the family is dispensable is only reflective of the broader notion of modern utopians and totalitarians that all mediating institutions which compete with the state or the collective for the individual's allegiance, such as the churches, neighborhoods, voluntary associations, unions, corporations, political parties, etc., should be abolished. These are viewed as restricting human freedom; the real result of restricting or abolishing them, of course, is complete state control over the individual and a genuine loss of liberty. Perhaps the family is hated most because it is the most universal and most durable of these institutions.

practices he or she wishes, including reasonable corporal punishment, should also be eliminated. Thirdly, child abuse should be treated as a criminal matter to be dealt with in regular courts, where accused persons have the full range of due process and other constitutional rights. Due process guarantees should also be established by statute for persons involved in any related matters which are more appropriately dealt with in juvenile court. For example, non-criminal neglect should perhaps receive a hybrid status under the law — not a criminal matter, but no longer treated as a civil matter — but with the accused person's constitutional rights fully protected. Part of the reform in this area should include permitting accused persons to waive secrecy in child abuse proceedings; sometimes the very thing needed to protect rights and guard against state abuse is the watchful eye of the public. Also, strict requirements should have to be met before state agencies can remove children from their homes. Children should not be removed, even temporarily, unless authorities can *conclusively* prove in a proceeding before an impartial judge that they are in danger. In the case of emergency removals, authorities should have to supply this proof to a judge within twenty-four hours, or automatically be required to return the child. Actually, perhaps Mrs. Pride's proposal is the preferred alternative to removing children: remove the *perpetrator*, as would be done with any criminal offense.[76] It follows also that records of unsubstantiated or false complaints should not be allowed to be retained by authorities. The statutory changes of the last several years which permit the admission into court of hearsay evidence and videotaped testimony and generally give the child the overwhelming benefit of the doubt against the accused should be repealed; child abuse should be dealt with like any other crime. Fourthly, safeguards should also be put in place to insure against manipulation of children by prosecutorial authorities, psychologists, and other

---

[76]See Pride, pp. 132-134, 144.

interrogators. Perhaps besides providing free legal counsel for needy accused persons in child abuse cases, we should also provide free psychologists and psychiatrists to counter the ones trooped in by the state.

Next, the laws should be changed to outrightly discourage and even make it risky for people to file false and malicious child abuse complaints. The laws should require something like "probable cause" — at least some threshold evidentiary requirements that seriously raise the likelihood that genuine abuse has occurred — before an agency has the authority even to commence an investigation. This should be the case because, after all, we are dealing with the natural rights of parents and with an intrusion into the most basic human institution, the family, and one of the most intimate of human relationships, that between parent and child. If someone makes a malicious or intentionally false complaint, he should be liable to suit in tort by the accused party. If a person has to face a trial, or even perhaps other legal proceedings, as a result of a knowingly false or malicious charge of child abuse and is exonerated, reversal of attorney's fees should be permitted. Generally, American law does not permit this, but exceptions have been made when a person is the victim of some particularly outrageous conduct.

Lastly, it is also time to reverse what Mrs. Pride calls the "one-sided liability" of the child abuse laws which make it "almost impossible to win a lawsuit when a child is removed [from his home] in error."[77] Social workers and/or state agencies can be sued or even criminally prosecuted for *not* removing a child from his home who afterwards is harmed or killed. They generally are immune from suit, however, when they wrongly remove a child, even without grounds and regardless of how much damage is done to the child or the parent-child relationship. It is time to correct this situation to insure that both parents and social workers and their agencies are treated fairly. Social workers and

---

[77]Pride, p. 81.

agencies should not be subject to suit or prosecution for nonremoval unless their conduct is clearly outrageous and/or in bad faith. They *should* be subject to suits by parents and legal guardians for wrongful removal, but only if they violate legal provisions — presuming the laws have been tightened up to prevent the easy removals which are now occurring — or act recklessly or maliciously. Prosecutional authorities should also be subject to suit if they act in such a manner, as was possibly the case in Jordan, Minnesota.

Finally, besides legal changes, there needs to be a restoration of common sense judgment — the rejection of which has distinguished modern times and thought — in the matter of childrearing and in this whole child abuse area. People should make it a point to investigate this issue and learn what child abuse is and what it isn't and how the laws have been misused. They should take the time to let their public officials and fellow citizens know they are displeased with the laws and their enforcement. They should also develop a proper understanding of what it means to "be thy brother's keeper," realizing that it does not imply the right to interfere in his childrearing practices except in extreme cases.

The suppression of parental rights through the child abuse laws is today a "silent tyranny"; one almost never notices anything about it in the media or in the speeches of public officials. An important reason for this is that it is not fashionable these days to be pro-family, at least not in anything but a superficial way that is really geared toward promoting some item on the agenda of the secular left, such as more welfare programs. In an era of rights, it is the area of rights that matters not at all. It is a tyranny nevertheless: one which Mrs. Pride says "threatens every North American Family."[78]

---

[78]This quote is from the long subtitle of her book: *Outrageous Facts About Child Abuse and Everyday Rebellions Against a System that Threatens Every North American Family.* She says "North American" because a portion of her book is dedicated to discussing the child abuse laws and enforcement in Canada too, where the situation is possibly even worse than here.

Index

A

abortion, 7, 10, 11, 24, 27, 34, 37, 40, 42, 49, 52-57, 59-61, 64, 67-68, 71, 73, 95, 99, 101, 112, 128, 147-148, 183, 187-188
  as encouraging child abuse, 188-189
  minors, access to without parental consent, 49, 59-66, 73, 111, 187
  right to (*see also* privacy, right of; right[s]), 54, 56-57, 59, 70, 73
  rights of father in, 49, 66-71, 148
  state funding of, 54
abortionist (physician in abortion), 55-57, 59, 66, 71
Adler, Mortimer, 185
adultery, 96, 98, 187
AIDS (Acquired Immunodeficiency Syndrome), 96, 99, 105
Akron v. Akron Reproductive Health Services, 56, 61, 64
Alabama, 82, 83, 84, 123, 127, 129, 130
  Department of Youth Services of, 125
alcohol abuse (*see* substance abuse)
alcohol, legal age to consume (*see also* substance abuse), 129-132
  effect on alcohol abuse, 129
Allen, James E., 103
American Bar Association, Family Law Section, 143
American Civil Liberties Union, 96
Amish, 90, 149
Amnesty Bill of 1872, 150
Anaheim, CA, 102
Arendt, Hannah, 41
Aristotle, 18, 33, 46
  Ethics of, 24-25
  Politics of, 18
  view of the family, 9
Augustine of Hippo, Saint, 24

B

Becerra, Rosina M., 160, 168
Becoming a Person program, 107
Bellotti v. Baird I, 60, 148
Bellotti v. Baird II, 60
Bennett, William J., 95, 96

Benziger Family Life program, 107
Berger, Peter, 151
Besharov, Douglas J., 139, 154-155, 167, 170, 171, 172, 179, 180-181
Bible, The, 40, 78, 86, 99, 100, 107
Bill of Rights, U.S. (*see also* Fifth Amendment, First Amendment, Fourth Amendment, Ninth Amendment), 146, 149, 150
birth control (*see* contraception)
Blackmun, Harry A., 60
Blaine Amendment, 79
Blits, Jan, 46
Bloomington case ("Infant Doe" case) (*see In re Guardianship of Infant Doe*)
Bloomington, IN, 58, 72
Boston, MA, 172
Brandwein, Paul, 16
Brennan, William, 47, 60, 80
Brown v. Topeka Board of Education, 46-47
Bruges, Belgium, 36
Bucharin, N., 17
Buddhism, 80
Burger, Warren, 60
busing, 7

C

California, 179n., 188
Calvinism (*see also* Protestantism), 190, 191n.
Canada, 101, 196n.
Cardinal Glennon Hospital, 171
Case and Comment, 155
Catholic Church (Catholicism), 29, 79, 93, 99, 100, 105, 106, 107, 108
  Charter on the Rights of the Family, 108
  Familiaris Consortio, 93
  1980 World Synod of Bishops, 108
  Pontifical Council for the Family, 107
Charter on the Rights of the Family (*see* Catholic Church [Catholicism])
chastity, 102, 105, 191
Chicago, IL, 107
child abuse and neglect (*see also* abortion, family, parental rights), 7, 11, 45, 47, 51, 62, 96, 106, 133, 137-146, 174, 177n.-178n., 181, 184, 188-190, 195
  adoptive parents and, 158

alleged in child custody
proceedings, 155
as caused by natural parents, 153,
157-158
corporal punishment as, 164-167,
170n.-171n., 189, 192-193
definition of, 138, 140-145, 154,
156, 158, 160-173, 192, 195
foster parents and, 157, 158, 177n.,
180-181, 188
frequently alleged in custody
battles, 160
hotlines for reporting, 159, 173, 192
innocent acts considered as, 158-
172
judges' understanding of, 172
media's portrayal of, 154, 156, 158,
178n.
not providing education as, 161-
163, 167
physicians' understanding as, 163-
164, 171
proposals for changes in laws and
practices to address, 192-195
reasons for overreporting of, 159-
173, 177n.-178n., 179, 189, 192
reliability of alleged victims'
accounts of, 176-179, 182, 186,
193
right to counsel for victim of, 139-
140
rights of persons accused of, 173-
179, 193-194
sexual, 155, 156, 158, 160, 164, 167,
175, 176, 177-179
social workers' understanding of,
164, 166-171, 181-184, 186-187
state agencies set up to address,
138-139, 167-168, 170, 172, 174,
179-183, 186, 189, 192-195
statistics about amount and nature
of, 154-159, 180, 181
statutes, 138, 155, 160-167, 171-179,
181, 185, 186, 187, 189, 190, 191n.,
192, 194-195
Child Abuse Industry, The (book), 156,
196n.
Child Abuse Prevention and
Treatment Act, 138, 161, 173
child custody proceedings, 155, 160
child labor, 140
Child Sexual Abuse Accommodation
Syndrome (*see* child abuse and

neglect, reliability of alleged victims'
accounts of)
children (*see also* child abuse and
neglect, domestic society, education,
family, juvenile delinquency, parents,
parental rights, parental duties,
reproduction, unborn child), 16, 27,
38, 46-47, 148-149, 184-186, 188-189,
192, 193
aggressive behavior in, 117-119
"best interests of" (legal standard),
60-62, 64-66, 73, 138, 142, 143-
146, 148, 150, 164, 166
defective, 41-42, 52-53, 71-74
legal requirements for
immunization, 140
legally protected rights and
interests of (*see also* "children's
rights," ideology of), 51-52, 59-66,
72-73
missing, 156-157
right to abortion (of minor girl)
(*see* abortion, minors, access to
without parental consent;
abortion, right to)
rights and dignity of subverted by
ruling legal doctrines, 71
suicides of, 7
"children's rights," ideology of, 45-46,
115, 133, 143, 148, 151, 189, 191
Christianity (*see also* Calvinism,
Catholicism, Protestantism), 9, 79,
81, 85-86, 94, 98, 99, 112, 163
fundamentalist, 81, 85, 105
civil society (*see also* state), 23, 27, 31,
34, 37-38, 40
as special educator, 33
common goods attained by, 32-33
end of, 32
good of, 33, 38
Civil War (U.S.), 79
*Cleveland Board of Education v.
LaFleur*, 88
coercion theory, 117-118
collectivism (*see also* communism,
Fascist party, liberalism, statism,
totalitarianism), 100, 102, 112
Congress of the International Union
for Freedom in Education (1953), 36
Congress of the United States, 48, 110,
121, 132
Cohen, Howard, 45
common good, 9, 19, 33, 35, 100

common law, 9, 50, 72, 135-136, 142-143, 146, 148, 151, 152
communism (*see also* totalitarianism), 17, 18, 41, 108, 152
conjugal society (*see also* marital relationship), end of, 20-23, 30, 42
Connecticut v. Manillo, 55-56
conscience, 15, 17
Constitution of the United States (*see also* Bill of Rights, U.S.; Due Process Clause; Fifth Amendment; First Amendment; Fourteenth Amendment; Fourth Amendment; Ninth Amendment; religion; right[s], constitutionally protected), 39-40, 49-51, 53-55, 64, 70, 83, 146, 150-151
   interpretation of, 51-53, 73, 89
contraception, 20, 46, 96, 99, 101, 109, 112, 127, 183, 187
   minors, access to without parental consent, 7, 42, 46, 105, 127-128, 187
Coulson, W.R., 188-189
Cuba, 152

D

D'Agostino, Robert J., 11, 162
Dallas, TX, 35
Danton, Georges Jacques, 15n.
Declaration of Independence, U.S., 39, 40
Defining Child Abuse (book), 160
Delaware Law School of Widener University, 7
Delaware, University of, 46
democracy, attitudes toward, 185
discrimination, race and sex, 190n.
divorce (*see also* family), 7, 41, 77, 155, 157-158, 160, 183-184, 187-188, 190
domestic society (*see also* conjugal society, divorce, end, family, marital relationship)
   as education, 32
   as nurturer of children, 36
   end of (purpose of), 20-26, 30, 32
   enemies of, 38
   properties of, 29-30, 37
Down's syndrome, 58, 72
drug abuse (*see* substance abuse)
Due Process Clause, 88

E

education,
   child neglect as indicated if parent does not provide, 161-163, 167
   duty of civil society with respect to, 33
   home, 85, 105-106, 162
   liberal arts, 96
   moral, 96, 98
   parental choice of children's, 11, 54, 77, 108
   parental duty to secure for children, 25, 77
   parental right to control children's, 26-31, 36-37, 54, 57, 65, 77-91, 101, 108, 111-112, 184-185
   purpose of, 35, 38, 84
   religious, 16, 54, 78, 84, 86, 90, 91, 96, 108, 149
   university-level, as faulty, 182
Education in Love program, 107
Education, U.S. Department of (*see* United States of America)
end (purpose) (*see also* family, man)
   of domestic society (the family), 20-23, 27
   of man, 18-19
   of organizations, 19
Equal Rights Amendment, 7
Establishment Clause (*see* religion, establishment of)
Ethical Culture, "religion" of, 80
euthanasia (*see also* infanticide; right[s], to die), 42, 50, 57, 59
existentialism, 40

F

Familiaris Consortio (*see* Catholic Church [Catholicism])
family (*see also* child abuse and neglect; children; "children's rights," ideology of; divorce; domestic society; end; juvenile delinquency; parental duties; parental rights; right[s]; state; substance abuse)
   Aristotle's view of, 9
   as educator (parents), 24, 26-28, 36, 54, 57, 77, 87, 91, 93, 108, 111-112, 136, 184-185

as essential and having an interest
in the upbringing of children, 22,
24-31, 36, 38, 88-90, 135-136, 192
as prior to other societies, 108, 151
attacked by utopians and
totalitarians, 192n.
common law and, 9, 50, 72, 135-136,
142-143, 148
common goods of, 32
competing views of, 7-8, 147-148,
150
damaged by abortion and
contraception (*see also* abortion,
contraception), 187
damaged by the sexual revolution,
187-191
definition of, 8, 137, 157
denigrated by "children's rights"
advocates, 16, 46
divorce and, 7, 41, 77, 155, 157
effect of law and legal system on,
119, 127, 130, 147, 152, 153
end of (purpose of), 20-23
government spending for programs
aimed at, 133, 195
importance of, 9, 93, 108, 112, 118,
134, 135, 153, 190-191
influence on deviant behavior of
children, 118
Judeo-Christian tradition and, 9
law and (*see also* abortion, child
abuse and neglect, education,
infanticide, juvenile delinquency,
sex education), 11
morality and (*see also* religion, sex
education, sexual morality), 8-9
nature of, 18, 40, 120, 150, 182
Plato's view of, 34-35
property and, 9
relationship to state, 8-11, 14-15,
27, 31-38, 47-48, 51, 54, 59-91, 94-
106, 108-113, 116-117, 119-134,
136-152, 153, 156, 167, 179-182,
184-186, 191-194
role of, 8, 32, 36, 136-137, 152
single-parent, 7, 137, 157
view of social workers of, 181-186
violence in, 137-138, 158, 167
family planning (*see* contraception)
Farrington v. Tokushige, 87
Fascist party (in Italy) (*see also*
totalitarianism), 17, 18, 152
father, rights of in abortion (*see*
abortion)

feminism, 189, 191
Fifth Amendment, 53
First Amendment (*see also* religion,
establishment of; religion, free
exercise of; state), 53, 62, 83, 89, 90,
111
Florida, 68, 181
fornication, 96, 99, 106, 188, 190
Founding Fathers (U.S.), 9, 51, 70
Fourteenth Amendment (*see also* Due
Process Clause), 50, 53-54, 87, 88, 146
Fourth Amendment, 53, 55, 175
Free Exercise Clause (*see* religion, free
exercise of)
freedom (*see also* liberty), 37, 38, 77,
88, 101, 192n.
religious (*see* religion, free exercise
of)
French Revolution, 15n.

G

Gagnon, Edouard Cardinal, 107
Gelles, Richard J., 146, 167, 170n.
genetic engineering, 27
Germany, Nazi (*see also* National
Socialist [Nazi] Party), 152
Gideon, 40
Ginsberg v. New York, 88
Giovannoni, Jeanne M., 160, 168
gnosticism, 97
God (*see also* Catholicism,
Christianity, Judaism, Protestantism,
religion), 8, 10, 16, 26, 28, 30, 40, 78,
80, 83, 85, 93, 100, 107, 186
government programs
aimed at family, 124, 128, 133, 195
damaging to family, 11, 119-120,
122, 125-131
ineffectiveness of, 11, 116, 119-127,
131
Gracey, Mr. & Mrs. Gerald (Gracey
case), 109
Grant, Ulysses S., 79
Greeks, ancient, 13
view of family life, 9, 13, 34-35
Green v. New Kent County, 46-47
Griswold v. Connecticut, 88
Guesde, Jules, 15n.

H

H.L. v. Matheson, 61
Hand, Brevard W., 82-83
Harris v. McRae, 56
Harvard University, 163
Hatch Protection of Pupil Rights
Amendment, 110-111
Hawaii, 87
Health and Human Services, U.S.
Department of (*see* United States of
America)
Health, Education, and Welfare, U.S.
Department of (*see* United States of
America)
heredity, as shaping children's
behavior, 119
Hitler, Adolph, 41
Holt, Rinehart and Winston basic
reading series, 81-82
Home School Legal Defense
Association, 85
home-school association (*see also*
parent-teacher association), 109
homosexuality, 96, 99, 107, 112
Hull, Thomas, 82
Humanist Manifesto I, 98, 100
Humanist Manifesto II, 98, 100
Humanist, The (magazine), 98

I

Illinois, 159n., 175
Supreme Court of, 141
incest (*see also* child abuse and
neglect), 138, 159n.
index crimes, 120-121
"Infant Doe" (Bloomington, IN), 58
"Infant Doe" Case (*see In re
Guardianship of Infant Doe*)
"Infant Doe" regulations, 72
infanticide, 7, 10-11, 41, 49-53, 58-59,
71-74, 188
Iowa, 143-144
In re Gault, 64, 139
In re Guardianship of Infant Doe, 58, 72
In re Quinlan, 57-58
Institute for Psychological Therapies,
177
intelligentsia, liberal American, 96, 100
Intercollegiate Studies Institute (ISI), 8
in vitro fertilization, 50, 71

J

Jehovah's Witnesses, 63
Jesus Christ, 86
John Paul II, Pope, 93, 94
Johnson, Eddie Bernice, 35
Judaism, 9, 29, 94, 98, 99, 100, 112
Justice, U.S. Department of (*see*
United States of America; Office of
Juvenile Justice and Delinquency
Behavior [OJJDP])
Juvenile Court Acts, 51, 62
juvenile delinquency (*see also* children,
family), 7, 10, 33, 115, 120-127, 131-
133, 139, 152, 164
alternative programs to address,
123-126
as addressed by juvenile justice
system, 121-127, 131, 133
prevention of, 121, 126-127
serious crimes, 125-126
statistics concerning, 120-121, 125,
129, 130
"status" offenses, 121-125, 131, 139,
140, 147
Juvenile Justice and Delinquency
Prevention Act, 121, 125, 126
effect of, 125

K

Kansas City Times, 155
Kant, Immanuel, 25
Kenniston, Kenneth, 45
Kirk, Russell, 98, 182
Kirkendall, Lester, 102
Klicka, Christopher, 85
Krason, Stephen M., 11
Kurtz, Paul, 98

L

law (*see also* abortion; Bill of Rights,
U.S.; child abuse and neglect;
common law; Constitution of the
United States; discrimination, race
and sex; Due Process Clause; family;
Fifth Amendment; First
Amendment; Fourteenth
Amendment; Fourth Amendment;
index crimes; juvenile delinquency;

legal positivism; parental duties;
   parental rights; right[s]; state), 190-
   191
Law Enforcement Assistance Agency
   (LEAA), 121-122
legal positivism (positivism), 40, 150,
   152, 182, 190, 191
lesbianism, 99
liberal arts (*see* education)
liberalism, 15, 18, 27, 100, 102, 104,
   107, 111, 133, 186, 195
libertarianism, 152
liberty (*see also* freedom), 9, 15, 54, 87,
   148, 192n.
life, right to (*see* right[s], to life)
Likoudis, James, 10
Locke, John, 9, 25
Loving v. Virginia, 88

M

Mahon v. Roe, 54
man (*see also* end), 27, 28, 36, 191
   end of (purpose of), 18-19, 31, 34
   nature of, 8, 14, 31, 34, 40, 43, 52,
      100, 107, 135, 152, 166
   relationship to God, 8
   relationship to moral order (*see
      also* religion, sexual morality), 8
   relationship to society, 8, 40
   reproduction of as end of domestic
      society (reproduction), 20-26, 42
Mann, Horace, 79
marriage (marital relationship) (*see
   also* conjugal society, domestic
   society, family), 29-30, 66-69, 88, 107,
   135-136, 142, 147, 148, 152, 184, 187
Marriage and Divorce Today, 155
Marshall, Thurgood, 47, 60
Marxism, 40
May v. Anderson, 88
Maryland, 178n.
Marzen, Thomas, 10
Massachusetts, 60-61, 78
   Supreme Judicial Court of, 60
Massachusetts Bay Colony, 78
masturbation, 99, 107, 109
materfamilias, doctrine of uterine, 70
McGraw, Onalee, 14n., 35
media (*see* child abuse and neglect,
   media's portrayal of; children,
   aggressive behavior in; sex education,
   media's role in)

Meiklejohn, Alexander, 18
mental illness, 16, 104
Meyer v. Nebraska, 54, 63, 87-88, 142
Michigan, 91
Minnesota
   level of child abuse/neglect in, 155
   Jordan, MN child abuse case, 177,
      195
Missouri, 59, 147, 162-163, 168
   House of Representatives Report
      on false child abuse reporting, 160
   child abuse statute, 161, 164, 178
Model Custody Act, 143
Model Rules for Juvenile Courts, 139
Mondale, Walter, 46
Montagu, Ashley, 16
Montesquieu, Baron de, 9
Moore v. East Cleveland, 88
moral relativism (*see also* legal
   positivism, situation ethics), 85, 100,
   105, 106, 182-183, 186-187, 190
Mothers Against Drunk Driving
   (MADD), 130
*Mozert v. Hawkins County Public
   Schools*, 81-82
Mussolini, Benito, 14

N

National Association for the
   Advancement of Colored People
   (NAACP), 47
National Center for the Assessment of
   Delinquent Behavior and Its
   Prevention, 126
National Center on Child Abuse and
   Neglect, 138, 154
National Education Association, 96
National Institute on Alcohol Abuse
   and Alcoholism, Division of
   Prevention, 97th Congress of, 129
National Parents-Teachers
   Association, 96
National Socialist (Nazi) party (see
   also Germany, Nazi; totalitarianism),
   17, 18, 152
natural law, 8-11, 18, 20-22, 24, 29, 37-
   42, 85, 94, 96, 98-101, 104, 112, 143,
   146, 150, 152, 153, 182, 186, 194
natural rights, 8, 9, 10, 22, 37-42, 94,
   112, 143, 146, 152, 153, 186, 194
"natural rights of parents doctrine" (in
   American law), 142, 144, 146

Nebraska, 54
Neuhaus, Richard John, 151
"New Bill of Sexual Rights and
    Responsibilities, A," 98, 99, 102
New Creation series (William C. Brown
    Co.), 107
New Kent County (VA), 46-47
New York State, 143, 146, 147
    Education Department, 103-104
    Health Law, 103
    Legislature, 103-104
    level of child abuse/neglect in, 154
    refusal to mandate sex education,
        103
1984 (novel), 41
1964 Civil Rights Act, 47
Ninth Amendment, 53, 146, 151
North America, 196
North Dakota, 91
Norwood v. Harrison, 88

O

Office of Juvenile Justice and
    Delinquency Prevention, U.S.
    Department of Justice (OJJDP), 125,
    126
Ohio, 11, 159n.
    child abuse/neglect statute, 161-167
    Juvenile Court Act of, 64
Oregon, 54
    Court of Appeals of, 142
Origins of Totalitarianism, The (book),
    41
Orwell, George, 41

P

parental duties (*see also* child abuse
    and neglect, education, family,
    Missouri, Ohio, religion), 23-26, 29-
    30, 34-35, 39, 42-43, 65, 77, 93-94,
    106-107, 117, 136, 190-191
parental rights (*see also* education,
    family, religion), 7-11, 14-18, 23-26,
    29-34, 36-37, 39-43, 45, 48, 49-75, 77,
    87-91, 93-94, 97, 101-109, 111-113,
    115-117, 119-120, 122, 126-129, 131-
    132, 136, 140-154, 156, 173-179, 181-
    186, 189, 190, 192-194
    under the U.S. Constitution, 51, 59-
        74, 81-84, 87-91, 149

parents
    as fit by nature for rearing and
        educating their children, 26-29,
        35-36, 38
    licensing of to have or rear
        children, 35-36
    unfitness of, particularly for rearing
        their children, 26
parents-teachers association (PTA)
    (*see also* home-school association),
    102, 109
paterfamilias, laws of ancient Rome, 70
Patterson, Gerald R., 117-119
Pennsylvania, 174n.
People for the American Way, 96
performance theory, 117
Philadelphia (PA), 163, 166
philosophy, perennial (*see also* natural
    law), 39, 98, 100, 101
Pierce, Dr., 16
Pierce v. Society of Sisters, 54, 63, 87, 88,
    89, 90, 111
Planned Parenthood, 105
*Planned Parenthood Association v.
    Ashcroft*, 56, 61
*Planned Parenthood of Central Missouri
    v. Danforth*, 59-61, 67, 70, 147
Plato, 13
    Republic, The of, 13, 34
    view of the family, 34-35
Pledge of Allegiance, 80
Poe v. Ullman, 88
pornography, 96, 99
Powell, Lewis F., 60-61, 88
pregnancy, out-of-wedlock, 95, 115,
    127
President's Commission on Law
    Enforcement and Administration of
    Justice, Report of, 141
Pride, Mary, 156, 158, 159n., 160n.,
    161-162, 164, 166n., 168, 170n., 171n.,
    173, 174, 177, 178, 179, 181, 184, 187,
    193, 194, 196
Prince v. Massachusetts, 80, 90
prison, as not rehabilitating criminals,
    126
privacy, right of(*see also* right[s]), 40-
    42, 53-54, 56-57, 66, 97, 107, 110, 112,
    140, 146, 150
procreate, right to (*see* right[s])
Progressive (magazine), 180
Protestantism (*see* also Calvinism,
    Christianity), 78-79, 84, 100, 105

Q

Quinlan Case (see In re Quinlan)
Quinlan, Karen Ann, 58

R

Rehnquist, William H., 60
religion (see also Buddhism, Calvinism,
  Catholicism, Christianity, Ethical
  Culture, Judaism, Protestantism,
  Secular Humanism)
    as basis for society, 102
    establishment of (see also state,
      view toward religion as mandated
      by U.S. Supreme Court), 78-81,
      82-84
    free exercise of, 82-83, 89-90, 111,
      163
    morality without, 97, 101
    need for, 191
reproduction, 18, 65, 66, 67-68, 71, 112,
  187
    as end (purpose) of domestic
      society (see domestic society, end
      of [purpose of])
Rhode Island, 67
Rice, Charles E., 11
Richmond, VA, 46
right(s) (see also abortion; Bill of
  Rights, U.S.; child abuse and neglect;
  common law; Constitution of the
  United States; discrimination; race
  and sex; Due Process Clause;
  education; Fifth Amendment; First
  Amendment; Fourteenth
  Amendment; Fourth Amendment;
  freedom; liberty; natural rights;
  "natural rights of parents" doctrine
  [in American law]; "New Bill of
  Sexual Rights and Responsibilities,
  A"; parental rights; privacy, right of;
  religion), 39-43, 150-152, 190
    as inhering in man because of his
      nature, 40
    common sense as basis for, 39
    constitutionally protected, 49-58,
      68, 71, 111, 173-176, 193
    human rights, international, 41
    of families as antedating the
      Constitution, 151
    of parents to control children's
      upbringing, 111, 149
    of pupils, 110-111
    to counsel (see also child abuse and
      neglect), 139-140
    to die, 49, 57
    to government services, 133
    to life, 40, 51-52, 73
    to marry and have offspring, 142,
      148
    to (of) privacy, 40-42, 53-54, 56-57,
      66, 97, 107, 110, 112, 140, 146, 150
    to procreate, 68, 70, 71, 148
    to seek "sexual gratification," 150,
      183
    to teach (of teacher), 87
    traditional, of Americans, 185
Rinn, Roger, 11, 135, 189
Robespierre, Maximilian, 15n.
Rochester, NY, 107
Rockefeller, Nelson, 103
Roe v. Wade, 49n., 55, 56, 65, 66, 67, 88,
  111, 127
Romans, ancient, 13, 70
    view of the family (see paterfamilias
      laws of ancient Rome)
Rome, ancient, 108
Rome, GA, 124

S

Sadlier Look at Life program, 107
Saint-Just, Louis Antoine Leon de,
  15n.
St. Louis, MO, 171
St. Petersburg, FL, 155
Scheinberg v. Smith, 68
schools
    boards of, 97, 127
    Christian day, 85-86, 105, 163
    compulsory attendance laws, 106,
      140, 184-185
    curricula, 11
    desegregation of, 7, 10, 46-48
    history of in U.S., 78-81
    influence on deviant behavior of
      children, 118
    moral issues treated in, 80-82, 96-97
    parental choice of for children, 11,
      36, 87-88
    parochial, 36, 86, 91, 94, 97, 101,
      106-107, 109, 113

prayer and religious elements in (*see also* religion, state), 79-82, 113
private (other than parochial), 36, 90, 97, 105
public, 78-84, 90, 94, 96, 97, 98, 101, 103-106, 112, 113, 127-128
public transportation of non-public school students, 7
School-Based Health Clinics (dispensers of contraceptives), 105
sex education in (*see* sex education)
values clarification programs in (*see* values clarification programs)
Seattle, WA, 126
Second Vatican Council, 77
secular humanism, 37, 79-81, 83-85, 94, 97, 98, 100, 101
Secular Humanism, "religion" of, 80, 111
Secular Humanism Declaration, A, 99
sensitivity training, 100
sex education (*see also* sexual morality), 7, 11, 80, 93-113, 127-128, 187
  as amoral, 94
  as reflecting secular humanism, 98-101
  clinical nature of, 106
  effect on the family of, 100, 127-128
  legal attack on, 109, 112, 113
  media's role in, 97, 102
  moral deterioration caused by, 95-96, 100, 112, 127
  perspective about sex presented in, 94
  sexual revolution and, 100, 127, 187
Sex Information and Education Council of the United States (SIECUS), 96, 102
sexology, 98, 102
sexual morality, 42, 94, 95, 96, 98, 99, 101-102, 104-107, 112, 128, 152, 188, 189
  and television, 96, 134
  ideology of sexual liberation (*see also* sex education, sexual revolution and), 99, 100, 115, 127, 183-184, 187, 191
  state regulation of, 99
  version of promoted in sex education programs (*see also* sex

education), 97, 101-102, 105, 127, 187
Sherman, Senator, 150
situation ethics (*see also* moral relativism, secular humanism), 100
Skinner v. Oklahoma ex rel. Williamson, 88
Slicke, William D., 155
Smith v. Board of School Commissioners of Mobile County, 82
social development theory, 135
socialism (*see also* collectivism, communism, liberalism, statism), 17, 107, 152
social learning theory, 117-119, 123, 124
Solzhenitsyn, Alexander, 97
Speno, Edmund J., 103
Stanley v. Illinois, 64, 88
state (*see also* civil society; family, relationship to state)
  as restricting parental authority, 37, 87-90, 105, 109, 115-117, 119-120, 122, 125, 127-131
  desirability for, of safeguarding parental rights, 31-33, 37, 122
  essential relationship of man as individual *and* as person to, 31
  in education, 14-18, 28, 31-36, 78-85, 87-88, 90, 96
  licensing of parents by (*see* parents)
  regulation of sexual morality (*see* sexual morality)
  relationship of individual to, 151, 192n.
  role in juvenile justice (*see also* juvenile delinquency), 123-125
  role of, 14, 32, 34
  view toward religion as mandated by U.S. Supreme Court, 80, 96, 109, 113, 152, 183
statism (*see also* collectivism, communism, Fascist party [in Italy], liberalism, National Socialist [Nazi] party, socialism, totalitarianism), 18, 107, 151, 184-186
Steubenville, OH, 11
Stevens, John Paul, 60
Stewart, Potter, 56, 60
subsidiarity, principle of, 31, 93-94
Supreme Court of the United States, 37, 40, 41, 46-47, 53-55, 59, 61-62, 64-65, 67, 69, 71, 77, 79, 80, 83, 86, 87-90, 111, 142, 148-150

surrogate parenting, 50, 71

T

Taoism, 80
television, effect of on minors (*see also*
  child abuse and neglect, children, sex
  education, sexual morality), 134
Texas, 159n.
Third World, 107
Thomas Aquinas, Saint, 14, 19, 21, 24,
  29, 46, 191n.
*Thornburgh v. American College of
  Obstetricians and Gynecologists*, 56
Time (magazine), 104-105
Torcaso v. Watkins, 80, 111
totalitarianism, 10, 14, 15, 17, 27, 34,
  41, 94, 107-108, 151, 186, 191, 192n.
tracheoesophageal fistula, 72

U

unborn child (*see also* abortion), 22,
  23, 24, 40-42, 49, 52-53, 66-67, 70, 75,
  128, 191
Uniform Juvenile Court Act, 139
Union of Soviet Socialist Republics
  (USSR), 41
  youth of, 97
United Nations, 36
  Universal Declaration of Human
    Rights, 36
United States of America (*see also* Bill
  of Rights, U.S.; Congress of the
  United States; Constitution of the
  United States; Declaration of
  Independence, U.S.; Founding
  Fathers [U.S.]; Supreme Court of the
  United States), 8, 11, 35-40, 45, 46,
  70, 78, 83, 87, 90, 94, 95, 98, 101, 111,
  112, 129, 133-134, 150, 152, 153, 157,
  170, 182-187, 194
  Department of Education, 95, 110
  Department of Health and Human
    Services, 168
  Department of Health, Education,
    and Welfare, 35
  Department of Justice, 121, 125
  law in (*see* law)
Utah, 67
utopianism, 191-192

V

values clarification programs, 7, 11, 100
Vatican Council II (*see* Second Vatican
  Council)
venereal disease, 96, 107, 115, 127

W

Warren, Earl, 47
Wall Street Journal, 155
Washington, DC, 133
Waters, Raphael T., 10, 39, 42, 43, 152,
  153, 182, 186
White, Byron R., 61
Whitehead, Alfred North, 84
Whitehead, Kenneth D., 10, 46
William C. Brown Co., 107
Williamsburg, VA, 46
Wisconsin, 89
Wisconsin v. Yoder, 63, 88, 90, 111, 149
Wolters, Raymond D., 10
World War I, 54, 96